Vojko Strahovnik, Bojan Žalec (Eds.)

Religion, Violence, and Ideology

Philosophy in Dialogue
Philosophie im Dialog

Edited by

Prof. Dr. Janez Juhant
(University of Ljubljana)
and
Ass. Prof. Dr. Vojko Strahovnik
(University of Ljubljana)

Volume / Band 3

LIT

Religion, Violence, and Ideology

Reflections on the Challenges of Postmodern World

edited by

Vojko Strahovnik and Bojan Žalec

LIT

Cover image: Anka Doblekar

Printed with the support of the Slovenian Research Agency.

This book is printed on acid-free paper.

Bibliographic information published by the Deutsche Nationalbibliothek
The Deutsche Nationalbibliothek lists this publication in the Deutsche Nationalbibliografie; detailed bibliographic data are available on the Internet at http://dnb.d-nb.de.

ISBN 978-3-643-90774-5

A catalogue record for this book is available from the British Library

Klosbachstr. 107
CH-8032 Zürich
Tel. +41 (0) 44-251 75 05
E-Mail: zuerich@lit-verlag.ch http://www.lit-verlag.ch
Distribution:
In the UK: Global Book Marketing, e-mail: mo@centralbooks.com
In North America: International Specialized Book Services, e-mail: orders@isbs.com
In Germany: LIT Verlag Fresnostr. 2, D-48159 Münster
Tel. +49 (0) 2 51-620 32 22, Fax +49 (0) 2 51-922 60 99, e-mail: vertrieb@lit-verlag.de
In Austria: Medienlogistik Pichler-ÖBZ, e-mail: mlo@medien-logistik.at
e-books are available at www.litwebshop.de

Acknowledgements

For the help and support in preparation of this book we would like to thank the reviewers Ciril Sorč and Rafal Smoczynski, to Janez Juhant, Dietmar Regensburger and European Academy of Sciences and Arts (Salzburg) – class VII. World Religions, to Valerija Japelj for proof-reading, and last but not least, to all the authors of the book.

We would also like to thank the Slovenian Research Agency (ARRS) for the financial support that enabled the preparation and production of this book and for the overall financial support of the research project *Religion as a factor of morality and intercultural dialogue* (ARRS J6–6851).

Vojko Strahovnik, Bojan Žalec
Ljubljana, September 2016

CONTENTS

INTRODUCTION

This book is a part of a wider project on the topic of the role of religion as a factor of ethics and intercultural dialogue. The contributions specifically focus on the interplay space between the phenomena of religion, ideology and violence, employing diverse approaches to key questions within it. The fundamental concepts for this endeavour are solidary personalism, dialogic universalism, opposing instrumentalism, solidarity, empathy, inter-culturality, and pluralism. Thus the main aim of the wider project can be captured as a multi-perspective investigation of the elements of culture, especially those which give it its dialogical and intercultural nature, and its relationship to religion(s).

Humanity is faced with grave challenges that require global and comprehensive answers to them, and perplexities surrounding the phenomena of religion, violence and ideology form a substantial part of these challenges. Essays in this book endeavour to contribute to the flourishing debate in this field. **Janez Juhant** after emphasizing some of the aspects of the rising role and impact of religion(s) in the global world forthrightly opens the question about religion as an origin of violence. His answer is that the processes of modernity have culminated on the one hand in the accumulation of controlled and directed political power that was most prominently perverted in totalitarian systems, and in the fading of proper ethical and social differentiations that enabled a healthy and cooperative society on the other. Religion-associated violence in such a context is more of a by-product of broader societal developments. In not diminishing the perspective of violence as an anthropological problem, proper solutions are to be found in establishing grounds for inclusive and dialogical communities. **Bojan Žalec** in an essay on radical Islamism and totalitarianism relates both phenomena and poses the initial thesis that aspects of radical Islamism are essentially totalitarian and at the same time have some distinctive characteristics. In particular, his investigation aims at explaining in which sense ideologies and groups of radical Islamism can be called totalitarian, and what form of totalitarianism they exemplify. In utilizing the analysis of totalitarianism by Hannah Arendt and the emphasis on elements of ideological thinking and terror (distinguishing practical terror and ideological terror), he demonstrates that radical Islamism harbours and exemplifies these basic elements. Žalec concludes with a proposal about our stance in opposing radical Islamism and opens some questions about deeper understanding of its prevalence (islamophobia). **Lenart Škof** in his essay on faith and humility turns his focus on two thinkers, namely Wilfred Cantwell Smith, a Canadian theologian and religious scholar, and Roberto Mangabeira Unger, a Brasilian-American pragmatist scholar, to propose a new insight into the understanding of the "theology of religions". In relating religion with central tenets of political and social ethics, he paves the way for emphasizing the importance of faith and humility as two central virtues of religion, establishing a space of relational, intersubjectivity-based ethics and peaceful coexistence among world religions. He concludes that for any religious individual it is of the greatest importance to understand the meaning of humility as a virtue and that this – in addition to recognition of the vulnerability of the other – is a key for the future theology of religions.

Branko Klun addresses the relationship between metaphysics and violence within the context of Vattimo's thought on postmodern democracy. Klun first elaborates the concept of metaphysical violence and goes on to demonstrate how Vattimo uses the facets of this concept to put forward a critique of the rigidity of liberal democracy. After delineating the key tenets of Vattimo's proposal of hermeneutic democracy as a model that rejects every metaphysical claim, allows a plurality of interpretations and disposes of the idea of metaphysical truth, Klun goes on to reflect on the proposal. He urges for rehabilitation of the notion of truth, as well as for a more positive interpretation of metaphysics. **Sandra Lehmann** discusses the key aspects of Milbank's ideas on violence. Lehmann starts first by outlining Milbank's thought that religion is not to be considered as inherently violent or as a source of violence, and that we should rather turn to secular modernity as the key constituent of the problem of violence. She proceeds by turning to the post-modern thought that can reveal the underlying complexities of our current situation, especially neo-liberalism, and then goes on to locate – together with Milbank – theological vision as a remedy for it. However, in the essay she proposes an alternative undertaking than Milbank's dualistic opposition of "ontology of violence" on the one side and "ontology of peace" on the other, and rather focuses on a more fundamental and realistic route of the common experience of suffering as a strategy to overcome violence. **Mario Wintersteiger** focuses on Georges Bataille and his writings on the sublime and the sacral in order to establish a firm and reflective anthropological basis for dealing with myth and violence. He utilizes Bataille's insights into the psychology of the

Fascist appeal to the masses and his meditations on a certain fascination with violence to point out that it can be politically dangerous to misjudge the power of myth. The interim conclusions are that a total "abolition of violence" is very likely impossible and that a complete "taboo on violence" can be dangerous. He concludes that small, controlled doses of mythology can have the effect of a beneficial poison (also in the sense of a catharsis, carried out through rituals, festivals, games etc.) that immunises people against most dangerous myths.

Nadja Furlan Štante deals with perplexities embedded within and surrounding the hierarchical supremacy and the battle for the (pre) power in terms of "power over" and domination between the genders. She locates that as a prominent origin of gender-based violence. Starting with the recognition that gender stereotypes and prejudices often contribute a considerable share in the preservation and creation of gender hierarchies, one can move to a profounder analysis of the understanding of the "power over" concept. She uses the methodology of the hermeneutic key of feminist theology in an attempt to warn of the danger and harmfulness of such negative gender stereotypes and prejudices. Pointing to the examples from Slovenian socio-religious sphere (which can be transposedly located also in other cultural contexts), she points to the significance of the logic of love against the logic of domination. The logic of domination that follows the principle of violence should be replaced with the logic of love, that goes beyond that and accentuates and joins together male and female gifts or diversities and does not assess them through the lens of superiority or inferiority. **Rok Svetlič** discusses the so-called radical political philosophy (A. Badiou, S. Žižek) in the context of philosophy of religion. He utilizes the former as a meta-position that enables the recognition of the structure of ideology and its affinity to violence. His main thesis is that certain ideological concepts are very similar to the understanding of the Being that was characteristic for the medieval Christianity (Hegel). He concludes by noting that we must reject radical political philosophy, especially at its criticism on democracy and human rights. **Vojko Strahovnik** discusses the notion of hospitality and the role of religions in relation to it. The notion of hospitality is becoming more and more present in the modern discourse on global ethics. In relation to the idea of global justice and the right to hospitality, he develops a notion of an agent of hospitality. Only a joint effort of these agents could pave the way for progress towards cosmopolitan justice, embodying the genuine, peaceful ethics of hospitality. Religious communities and religions in general are also important agents of hospitality. One can contrast "hostility" as the violent potential of religion with "hospitality" or the healing potential of religion as the antidote for it, and relates both to imagination as the resource and mechanism that shapes our attitudes and actions. Religions have a vital role in establishing hospitality and in the process of overcoming new religious intolerance by creating a context of sympathetic imagination and respect.

The editors

Ljubljana, September 2016

JANEZ JUHANT: FROM IDEOLOGICAL PRESSURE TO THE SOUND POLICY OF COOPERATION

Introduction

The Age of Enlightenment stressed a pejorative role of religions in society. Now we seem to be facing a turning point: religion is coming back and this includes a more objective view on religion in the socio-political sphere. The political life in the European countries in the Middle Ages was very much influenced by religious observance. The fulfilment of religious duties was the constitutive part of the functioning of the societies and states. The political absolutism was prevented by the division on worldly and celestial hierarchy. Liberal tensions in the modern monarchies (like Austro-Hungarian) eroded this Christian equidistant order; the politics should be free from all religious and Church's influences. The liberal tensions questioned firmly established societal order excluding the religious relation of society. E.g. Austrian Emperor Josef II. (1741-1790) usurped the Catholicism just for his absolutist imperial purposes. The Enlightenment tensions to unification opened the tension of universalisation. Our thesis is that this was not a religious but an imperial liberal-political universalisation, combined with the tension to unification and polarization of different worldviews and religious points of view. We have witnessed a global political development in the direction of the concentration of the whole political power in particular political entities and persons. This culminated in the totalitarian systems, which distorted classic human, cultural and ethical order (Bauer 2014). In extreme-revolutionary circumstances, the traditional values were suspended and – in communist countries – "non-values" (laying, stealing, murder) prevailed.

As a consequence, the post-totalitarian order still has tendencies to unification and exclusion of democratic values. The European liberal political praxis, especially in the last century, has influenced the so called Islamic totalitarian tendencies in the Near East, which has culminated in Al-Qaeda, Islamic State and in other quasi-political forms of modern terrorism. The question arises whether the grounds of their destructive powers are religious or (quasi-)political, derived from modern totalitarian residues and delusions. Sachs (2015, 100) claims that "violence exists because we are social animals. We live and find our identity in groups conflicts. They fight over the same resources: food, territory, and other scarce goods. (...) Religion plays a part in this only because it is the most powerful source of group identity the world has yet known. Every attempt to find a substitute for religion has resulted in even more violence." Man is naturally prone to violence and only dialogue among different positions can clear our human reality. The way toward peace among the politics and religions is an open society (Popper 1945/1966). Religions can contribute to the sound political development and peace. The real question is not whether God should be referred to in the constitution of EU, but who is ready to implement Christian or other religious values in public policies. Cavanaugh (2010) suggests that Christians can form Eucharistic communities that are a Christian order of persons, solidarity and subsidiarity. To live means to live together and to share and to dialogize, to build Eucharistic communities.

Interests for religion(s)

"Around 1975 the whole process [of secularization] went into reverse. A new religious approach took shape, aimed not only at adapting to secular values but at recovering a sacred foundation for the organization of society—by changing society if necessary. Expressed in a multitude of ways, this approach advocated moving on from a modernism that had failed, attributing its setbacks and dead ends to separation from God. The theme was no longer *aggiornamento* but a 'second evangelization of Europe': the aim was no longer to modernize Islam but to 'Islamize modernity'. Since that date this phenomenon has spread throughout the world." (Kepel 1994, 2)

A difficult problem is that contrary to the so called postmodern paradigm (many personal stories) we are facing with the new tension for polarization and unification (Bauer 2014). In the "revival of religions", there are often scapegoats for these new tensions and their consequences (war, refugees, environmental problems). A general question arises: Which are the basic values in these societies? In modernity, they were influenced by exclusive and quasi-religious worldviews, supported by the phenomenon of unification (universalisation) and exclusion of others. The exclusion and pugnacious relation among different streams tended to the pan-movements and totalitarianism (Arendt 1951). It all culminated in totalitarian regimes, but their downfall did not end those tendencies, since imperialistic and pan-tensions have remained. Ignoring the importance of religions for societal life is a part of those processes and now we have an opportunity to overcome the residues of a one-sided view (Comte, Marx, Nietzsche, liberal and Marxist ideologies, Freud).

Naive, only partially grounded perceptions mark religions as violent. Bauer stresses that in comparison to the Islamic culture, the Western society had 'religious wars' (Bauer 2014, 345 ff). Such one-sided evaluation of religions and intrusive and violent handing over of religious convictions were and still are a part of imperialistic policy of the European colonial powers. They remain as a negative residuum. In the communist countries, that was accompanied by a violent campaign against religious consciousness. The main point of revolutionary propaganda was that religion is violent, oppressive and destructive. It was propagated that religions should be completely apolitical (as a 'personal thing'=faith) and were presented as having a negative role in society. These residues remain in the post-communistic time. All this causes negative reactions among the bearers of religious belief.

'Sociotheology' and 'religious violence'

The growing role of religion, the empty spiritual space on the on hand and the importance of Islam today on the other increase the critical rethinking of the role of religions in societies. Sheikh (2015, 134) states: "In most cases the motivations of political actors who employ religious vocabulary or draw on religious imaginary are neither fully religious nor secular. Rather, they represent a blend that challenges any clear-cut division. Research on activists involved in acts of terrorism show that they simultaneously understand their acts in religious terms and as a part of struggles for peace, justice and better socio-political order. For them, there is no 'secular' distinction between defending faith and defending a just sociopolitical order since the latter is a part of their religious vision."

Thus, religion needs to be acknowledged as an important part of socio-political reality of man. Next, the question arises what kind of religion is meant here and if it is really violent a priori. The violent aspects of Islam (like that of Christianity) were and still are shaped by the neoliberal-political purposes. If we turn to socio-political reality of 21st century we must admit that religion is not very influential in comparison to other non-religious worldviews/ideologies, but the role of religions is increasing. Sheikh admits that by saying: "This does not mean that worldviews are only significant when it comes to understanding violent acts committed by adherents of religious traditions. Worldviews are also entry points to understanding 'secular violence' acted out as a part of a secular vision of the world, and also relevant for debates that are not about behaviour at all" (134–5). Sheikh admits that there are many such temptations in Islam (Taliban), Judaism (Zionists) and Christianity (Christian abortion clinic bombers), Sikhs and Hindu nationalists in India, and even Buddhism in several countries of the Far East. Sachs speaks about the return of religion: "The religion that has returned is not the gentle, quietest, eirenic and ecumenical form that, in the West, we had increasingly come to expect. Instead it is religion at its most adversarial and aggressive, prepared to battle with the enemies of the Lord, bring the apocalypse, end the reign of decadence and win the final victory for God, truth and submission to the divine will …) Undeniably, though, the greatest threat to freedom in the postmodern world is radical, politicised religion. It is the face of altruistic evil in our time" (2015, 14).

But Sheikh is convinced that the theological point of view has been banished from sociological analyses until now and it is necessary to place it in the new circumstances. She names it socio-theology: "It also requires understanding the relation between the people who share a certain worldview and the social and power structures of the world around them" (Sheikh 2015, 138). This implies the "concentric circles of social realities, which coalesce (*coueles*) with particular epistemic worldviews" (139). There is a methodological question which authority underpin the epistemic worldviews and "how to measure the impact of an epistemic worldview turn to explain why only some of those who share an epistemic worldview turn to actual violence" (140). There is a need to be empathic to understand that there can be a political and religious rationale behind 'their' violence just as 'we' have in war and other situations (140). According to her, it is very important immediately to react to religious violence.

Non-violent Islam?

Bauer in his book *The culture ambivalence. Different story of Islam* analyses the religious and the socio-political tendencies respectively in the development of Islamic culture. There is no natural tendency that

Islam as such is the basis of unification of society and the cause of violence. Islamisation as a totalitarian process is caused by political circumstances of the modernity, which made possible the so called "islamisation of Islam" (Bauer 2014, 167). These tendencies reflect that "the problematic relation between religion and politics was influenced by something totally new – an experience of modernity" (Fradkin 2013, 123). There was an openness in the early Islamic societies and the theologians, philosophers and jurists pleaded for ambiguity, which means the differentiation of society. The political and the religious roles were not necessary combined or unified. This unification is a product of modern political and Western oriented simplification of Islam and projection of the Western liberal-imperialist tendencies in the Islamic political reality.

In comparison with this modern socio-political result, the sources of Islam in the first centuries were open and dynamic. This is the case for the interpretation of Koran and hadith (the explanations of Koran). The sexual life was not – as among Christians – regulated by the natural law. This made possible a more liberal sexual life in these communities. The much more decisive thing is an open socio-political discourse. Scientists (jurists, theologians, sociologists) and poets defended different accesses to reality. There is not only (one) religious world in Islam but from the beginning of the Islam the world has been differentiated. The places of others, especially of Jews and Christians, were positively defined so that the 'stranger' was no stranger and the other was better integrated as it was the case in the Western (Christian) societies. Jews were in Europe regularly much more persecuted than they were in Islamic countries. Only in the last centuries – according to Bauer – under the influence of the Western political and imperial tensions, the evaluation of Islam in the socio-political reality of modernity and the unification of Islam took part. The Islamic society has been more and more taking over aspects of the Western unification of life. This caused militant relations among different worldviews (religions). The reasons were not in the first place religious, but socio-political.

The modernity in Christian and Islamic societies

According to Bauer, there were no religious wars in Islam as there was among Christians at the beginning of the New Age. But he admits that the tensions towards unification are not the consequences of Christianity but of the liberal tensions in modernity. Liberal society of modernity tended towards unification (Toulmin) and exclusion of religions (Sachs). The dogmata against the Christian theology caused the dogmatisation in the Church and in the society (Toulmin 1990, 134). It began with the assassination of French king Henry IV (1610). In a sense, the second revolution of modernity with violent revolutions was a contra-revolution in comparison with the Renaissance. But in reality the real cause of these perturbations in the modern society were mostly the liberal and national political and societal streams, which had much more influence than Christian religions in the early modern times. The liberal societies tended to exclude the Catholic (and Protestant: Prussia) Churches from the society. This caused polarisation. The Churches were caught in the liberal struggles between 'ancient regime' on one side and the liberal bourgeoisie and the socialistic workers on the other. The Islamic societies especially of the Near and Middle East were involved in these circumstances too. Liberal nationalism caused the raise of national state. Bauer demonstrates this with an example of Turkey. At the begining of 20th century, in Turkey there were about 25% non-Islamic population but nowadays there remained only few. The genocide on Armenian people in 1915 is a part of the rise of the Turkish nationalistic state (Bauer 2014, 313).

'Religious violence'

To understand the origins of the so called religious conflicts it is very useful to consider the observations of Cavanaugh on religions and violence in his book *Myth of Religious violence. Secular Ideology and the Roots of Modern Conflict*. He argues, "that in 'Western' societies, the attempt to create a transhistorical or transcultural concept of religion that is essentially prone to violence is one of the foundational legitimating myths of the liberal national-state. The myth of religious violence helps to construct and marginalize a religious Other, prone to fanaticism, to contrast with the rational, peacemaking secular subject" (4). According to Cavanaugh the concept of religion was and still is changing and because of it we do not have a universal concept of religion. But for many, religion always includes something irrational, fanatical, and violent, "to legitimate the coercive measures against the Other" (5). According to those authors, there is a difference among religions and secular ideologies, but surprisingly the "former are essentially more prone to violence... more dangerous" (6), are "absolutist, divisive, irrational" (8) as are nationalisms, Marxism, capitalism, and liberalism. Cavanaugh opposes the general terms like 'religious violence', 'West' (e.g. in the sense of Huntington 1993, 192: "West and the rest"), 'religion', 'religious', 'secular'. Then he establishes that the contributions of those authors on diverse topics like history, politics are good and "have important insights to share on origins of violence", but dealing with the category of religion they fail. He asserts so far: "The idea that religion has a peculiar tendency toward violence must be investigated as a part of ideological legitimization of the Western national-state (…) The rise of the modern state did not usher in a more peaceful Europe, but the ascendency of the state did accompany a shift in what people were willing to kill and to die for. *Dulce et decorum est/pro patria mori* would take on normative status. I argue that legends regarding wars of religion are not simply objective history, but are an ideological accompaniment to shifts in Western configurations of power, especially the transfer of lethal loyalty to the emergent state"(12).

Cavanaugh proposes to analyze the wars through the last centuries to show that most of them were combined with the rise of the modern states. "Historians generally acknowledge – as political theorists do not – that other factors besides religion were at work in the wars of religion. These factors are political, economic, and social"(11). Cavanaugh asserts that it is almost impossible to separate these reasons for wars one from another. Religious factors were involved but others factors are equally important. He shows that 'religious wars' were actually wars for political domination in modern Europe. Cavanaugh asserts three types of arguments in relation to religious violence. The first one is that religion is absolutist (18). The second one is that religion is divisive, which means "the indictment of religion is based on religion's tendency to form strong identities exclusive of others …" (26), as Martin Marty and others claim. For our purposes, the last type which posits that 'religion is non-rational' (17) is important. The final argument is shared by Parekh, Selengut and Appleby, who try to show that this was implemented in the wars of former Yugoslavia. This type of argument supposes an absolutism of religion, but argues that religions have irrational residues (42–54).

The modern delusion

The complex circumstances of modernity caused several deviations of societal life. They influenced one-sided sociological observation of these phenomena; we can speak about the so-called 'modern' myths, which include scape-goating combined with an illusion to solve these problems by escaping reality. The former Slovene communist leader (son of very influential perpetrator of revolutionary crimes) said that they (communists) were lucky to hold Catholicism out of schools, which means no integration of religious education or any religious values. Thus in Slovenia there is still no dialogue about basic societal values. Despite the prevailed postmodern dialogical paradigm, modern myths are returning and forms of reduced views on reality are forming a problem of delusion. The reality could not be disclosed (*alétheia*) without a sincere dialogue. There are always tendencies of totalization, which means a reduced view of reality. This is the case with modern myths of the machine-technic and of the scientific development (Virilio 1989) or of the ideological totalization in the totalitarian systems. There are many delusions that make difficult to see the genuine problems, e.g. media delusions, delusion of status, political delusions (myth of the state, Cavanaugh 2010), delusions of the past and historical truth, colonial delusions, etc. To clear out these delusions, we must come to the core of our being – a mystical task, which can be performed only through sinverity. This task could be difficult to reach without a dialogue with the last ground of our being, God. Cavanaugh speaks about three myths that are the consequence of the modern liberal state: (1) the myth of the state as a saviour; (2) the myth of a civil society; (3) the myth of the globalization of Christianity; and one can add a fourth – the myth of violent Islam. (1) We are faced with the problems of functioning of EU and other political entities. We have to cultivate dialogue about these problems and to overcome the scapegoating. (2) Religion can't be simply replaced by the myth of civil society. The religious perception of society is grounded in the anthropological basis of man and must be regarded as important. (3) It is difficult to speak just of globalized Christianity as a saviour of the world; we have to admit the challenging processes of dialogical implementing of religious values in globalized world. (4) The myth of Islamic globalization as a liberal political process and the contribution of Islam to the world dialogue are important (Bauer 2014, Küng 2007).

The differentiation

Bauer is advocating a strong differentiation of society as a way to freedom and acceptance of others. How to come to a new ambiguity (differentiation) after the era of totalitarianisms and other imperialistic unifications and totalising globalizations? In my opinion the way to it is proper understanding of religion and politics in their roles in society. Habermas (2013) and Joas (2013) took different positions regarding this issue. Joas argues that we should focus on human rights, which safeguard basic relations among persons in the state. Habermas argues that this is not enough. We need the illumination of God to order our earthly things. This is a mystical position. Its tradition teaches us to be open for the deeper grounds of our being and to overcome the illusions of our daily life. Dialogue opens us for the sources of our being. In the dialogue between Indian and German theologians many of them are arguing that ethical and spiritual work are necessary presuppositions for the overcoming of religious and other differences. Jeyaraj is speaking about the spirituality of the Co-Pilgrim and acceptance of the Outsider (2013, 258; 265).

Interreligious dialogue requires a spiritual and ethical cooperation, including a very complicated exchange of symbolic structures. The most important part of this is not simply the exchange of words but emotional communication. Obstacles in this emotional exchange – such as parental or other relational violence – seriously damage people's symbolic ability. On the other hand good communication is the foundation of a happy life for individuals and supportive for *the art of life* of individuals and societies to overcome the will to power with the will to life (Sachs 2015, 252ff). Dialogical cultural exchange as a human creative process preserves humanity in its core and opens the paths of human creativity. Violent, authoritative or even totalitarian patterns hinder normal human development. A living dialogue is a way to overcome all these delusions and appearances of the modern way of life. MacIntyre (2006, 111) speaks about dialogical "conversational justice". Only dialogically, we can approach to (our) history in such a way that it is possible to establish the conditions to meet differences and in presence of mind get the real human ground. The religious substance can support the opening of the real grounds of humanity if we are ready for sincere dialogue among religions and among political entities (Küng 1990).

REFERENCES

Arendt, H. 1951. *The Origins of Totalitarianism*. New York: Schocken.

Bauer. T. 2013. *Kultura dvoumnosti. Drugačna zgodoivna islama [The culture ambivalence. Different story of Islam]*. Ljubljana: Krtina.

Cavanaugh, W. T. 2009. *The Myth of Religious Violence. Secular Ideology and the Roots of Modern Conflict*. Oxford: UP.

Cavanaugh, W. T. 2010. *Theopolitical Imagination*. London/New York: TT Clark LTD.

Fradkin, H. 2013. Die lange Suche nach dem Islamischen Staat. Religion und Politik im Islam und die Dynamik der Gegenwart. In: Graf, F. W.; Meier, H. (eds.) *Politik und Religion,* München: Beck, 121–161.

Habermas, J. 2013. Politik und Religion. In: Graf, F. W.; Meier, H. (eds.) *Politik und Religion,* München: Beck, 281–300.

Huntington, S. 1993. If No Civilisation. What? Foreign Affairs *72. 192:* https://www.foreignaffairs.com/articles/global-commons/1993-12-01/if-not-civilizations-what-samuel-huntington-responds-his-critics. Accessed 12 10. 2015.

Jeyaraj, A. 2013. *From Dialogue to Co-Pilgrim,* in: Dausner, R.; Eck, J. (eds.) *Theologien in ihrer cultureleln Prägung. Beiträge zum interreligiösen Dialog in Indien und Deutschland,* Regensburg: F. Pustet, 247–266.

Joas, H. 2013. Säkularisirung und Entsakralisierung. Politik und Religion. In: Graf, F. W.; Meier, H. (eds.) *Politik und Religion*, München: Beck, 259–285.

Küng H. 1990. *Weltehtos*. München: Piper.

Kepel, G. 1994. *The Revenge of God: The Resurgence of. Islam, Christianity and Judaism in the Modern World*. Cambridge: Polity Press.

Sheikh, M. K. 2015. '*Sociotheology:* The Significance of religious Worldviews'. In: Herrington, L.; Mackay, A.; Haynes, J. (eds.) *Nations under God. The Geopolitics of Faith in the Twenty-First Century.* Bristol: E-International Relations Publ, 134–143.

MacIntyre, A. C. 1999. *Dependent Rational Animals: Why Human Beings Need the Virtues*. Chicago: Open Court.

Popper, K. 1945/1966. *Open Society and its Enemies* I II. Princton: UP.

Sachs, J. 2015. *Not in God's Name.Confronting Religious Violence.* London: Hodder&Stoughton

Toulmin, S. 1994. *Kosmopolis. Die unerkannten Aufgaben der Moderne.* Frankfurt am Main: Suhrkamp.

Virillo, P. 1989. *Die Sehmaschine*. Berlin: Merve.

BOJAN ŽALEC: RADICAL ISLAMISM AND TOTALITARIANISM

1. Radical Islamism is a form of Western totalitarianism with some special own characteristics

We use the term *radical Islamism* (hereafter RI) to denote certain leaders, theorists and their doctrines respectively (for instance Wahhab, Qutb, Faraj, bin Laden, Zawahiri), and certain movements, groups or organizations (like Al Qaeda[1], ISIS etc.). There is a significant similarity between Western totalitarianism and radical Islamism at the ideological level and from the aspect of their socio-political origin and genesis. From the last aspect we can mention here the transformation of rural societies into urbanised, the confrontation with modernity, non-capability of the actual socio-political establishment to face the societal problems, and also the feeling of redundancy and senselessness which were created by industrialisation and urbanisation. All these factors triggered very similar effects in the Islamic world as they caused them in Europe of the 18th, 19th and 20th century. At the legal, philosophical and political level the similarities – which are most worth of concern – between legal and political-philosophical ideas are preferring collective over individual, the need to reinforce man to be free, and the arbitrary fabrication of imagined future and past utopia (Suurland 2009, 271).

Our main hypothesis is that radical Islamism is a form of Western totalitarianism with some special own characteristics. If this is true then the consequences of Al Qaeda and related movements for the Islamic world and for the multicultural West are very different then if these terroristic movements were only practically oriented, as for example ETA (ibid.).

What is the "essence" of totalitarianism? We can answer to this question with the help of the theory of totalitarianism of Hannah Arendt. The key terms in her definition of totalitarianism are i*deological thinking* and *terror*. She defined totalitarianism as a "system of government whose essence is terror and whose principle of action is the logicality of ideological thinking" (Arendt 1951 (hereafter OT), 398). Ideological thinking

---

[1] For the ideological background and the corresponding texts, respectively of Al Qaeda see Ibrahim (ed.) 2007.

is characterised by logicality (from basic premise to utopia). What is logicality of ideological thinking? Let as quote Arendt's own words:

> "Ideological thinking orders facts into an absolutely logical procedure which starts from an axiomatically accepted premise, deducing everything else from it; that is, it proceeds with a consistency that exists nowhere in the realm of reality" (OT, 471).

So we can start the analysis of a particular totalitarian thought by pointing to its basic premise. If we turn our attention to Nazism and Communism (Arendt in her *Origins of Totalitarianism* accepted only Nazism and Stalinism as true examples of totalitarianism) we find the following: In Nazism – its purification of the race can be interpreted as the answer to the chaos of the World – the basic premise is that the aim of history (Law of Nature) is a prevalence of the Arian race. A similar role as race in Nazism was played by class in the communistic doctrine(s): the aim of history (Law of History) is the achievement of Communism which will be carried out by the victory of proletariat.[2] Both movements have derived all the necessary conditions for the creation of utopia. The all-explaining premise which is the foundation of any totalitarian ideology was understood as »the law of nature" or "the law of history". The mechanism by which this premise transforms the world is regarded as some kind of "the law of movement" (Suurland 2009, 273). "Unfortunately" the process of reaching of the Arian dominance/purification of the world or establishing of Communism can last thousands and thousands of years so it should be accelerated. According to Hitler and Lenin a necessary part of this acceleration is killing of unfit persons. As such it is, according to the same doctrines, morally justified. Moreover, every action can be considered in the light of this new "morality". This thinking was connected with the radically new conception of freedom from which it follows that we must apply the law and its acceleration to all areas. Therefore, we must erase also the boundary between private and public. All this leads to a totalitarian movement. Everything is subjected to the goal to bring humanity in harmony with the ideal. We are dealing with the universal redemption of humanity by its purification. This is carried out by merciless application of logic to axiomatic premise, and by modern ways of social engineering.

---

[2] As Marx and Engels (2008, 9) wrote in the *Communist Manifesto*: "The history of hitherto existing societies is the history of class struggles".

2. Rationalization of terror, function of terror, kinds of totalitarian terror

In the frame of the academic debate on totalitarianism, an important subject is the function of terror. Some of the most reputable researches of totalitarianism (for instance Friedrich & Brzezinski (1966)) claim that terror is not a definitional characteristic of totalitarian regimes, while some other scholars claim just the opposite (Arendt (1951, 1970[3]), Havel (1985), Killingsworth (2012)). In a certain sense, this discussion is interesting only as far as we deal with firmly established totalitarian states. Radical Islamic movements do not belong to this class. With the exception of ISIS we are dealing with the movements without monopoly on power, and even without particular national base for operation. Often they are transnational oppositional movements. But on the other hand, the reflection on terror can help us to better understand also these movements.

There are two dimensions of totalitarian terror: practical terror and ideological terror. When the monopoly and stability are achieved, the practical terror is put to the backseat and the ideological terror steps in front.

---

[3] Arendt later (after OT) distinguished – in her essay *On Violence* (1970) – between violence and terror (as total terror). Terror, not violence, is the characteristics of totalitarianism. Martinjak (2016) nicely summarised (see especially pages 83-84) the distinction between them from the following aspects: 1. demonstration of clear form; 2. the validity and meaning of laws; 3. characteristic types of government and principles of people's action; 4. activity or passivity of people; 5. role of people; 6. community and bonds, relationships between people; 7. role for political field. The distinctions are the following (violence/terror): 1. one : all / one man in gigantic dimensions; 2. positive laws or arbitrariness (in case of tyranny); some people rule, some obey / totalitarianism; terror and ideology; 3. tyranny, despotism; fear, suspicions / totalitarianism; terror and ideology. 4. active or passive / passive; 5. using and accumulating instruments to subordinate other people / people are superfluous, they are only executers; 6. no need for them, violence is realized through means / high stage of atomization, bonds between people are destructed; 7. (dangerous) means of politics / destruction of politics in Arendt`s terms. The third main concept which Arendt compared to violence and terror (in the above regards) is power (see ibid.). In the second dimension in the case of power there are positive laws, people are supporting them and consenting to them. Regarding the third we deal with republic, monarchy, democracy and honour, virtues etc.

This means a coerced fabrication of utopia. This is at the same time *differentia specifica* of totalitarianism. There are three important observations we can make about the totalitarian ideological terror. First: The main aim of totalitarianism is realization of the law of nature or history respectively (not of the will of people). We are dealing with this or other revelation, with transcendental or secular "religion" which however is untouchable and which leads to prohibition of questioning and non-belief. The system is justified by its construction. The possibility of questioning of the system as such is not acknowledged, and that the form of science is a system must be assumed as being beyond all questions (Arendt, OT, 274). The main aim of totalitarianism is not the realisation of the will of people, but rather the transformation of the reality in the image of the totalitarian movement's own ideology, the realization of the law of nature. As Arendt notes in OT the terror is a realization of the law of movement. The aim is to enable the forces of the nature or of the history to freely flow through humanity without being hindered by any form of human spontaneity. Enemies are not only those who oppose the ideology, but rather all who are not its perfect embodiment. The sole act of thinking by one's own head and for oneself is the act of trait. Second: The sole existence of the world outside the totalitarian universe opposes the truth of totalitarianism. The totalitarian regimes most fear of non-totalitarian reality which proves their incompleteness. Thus Leon Trotsky – in his book *Permanent Revolution*[4] – wrote that the completion of socialist revolution inside the national border is inconceivable. Socialist revolution which starts in the national frame develops at the international level and finishes at the worldly, global level. Thus a socialist revolution becomes a permanent revolution: its completion is achieved only by the definitive and final victory of the new society on the entire planet. Totalitarian terror thus extends not only to non-totalitarian world but also to those subjects inside totalitarianism which are not indoctrinated enough as well. Those who are enemies are not enemies – at least not all of them – because they are some kind of real opposition, but rather according to the ideological key, by ideological necessity. Third: No failure or problems on the side of totalitarian movements or systems (regimes, states) is explained by (inherent) drawbacks of ideology and of the upon it built system, but rather by (external) enemies, i.e. sabotages, conspiracies and

---

[4] For the (Communist) theory of permanent revolution see also Roberts 2014.

counter-revolutionary activities. These three points imply that totalitarian revolution is a permanent war. Since the utopia will never be realized there will always be the need to invent an enemy, since otherwise this would mean that ideology itself is wrong. Totalitarian *raison d'etre* is in the future utopia. Its primal connection with the present times is identification and elimination of the enemy which harms the movement or regime no matter whether he is a Jew, a capitalist, or something else. Every totalitarian movement has passed through this process of identification and elimination of the enemy because this is the logical necessity of the totalitarian paradigm. The fields of death, Gulags and gas chambers: it was not the individual guilt that mattered but the ideological terror; its aim was the releasement of the forces of nature and history, respectively.

In the conclusion we may stress the following findings: we should distinguish the practical or utilitarian terror from the ideological one. Not only totalitarian systems are marked by the first. Yet the second one – to the contrary – is a characteristic only of the totalitarian systems because it is a consequence of totalitarian ideology, and the need of totalitarian systems which are founded upon it. Besides, the totalitarian revolution is a condition of a permanent war against reality. Everybody must be subjected to the power of totalitarian movement because it is a movement against freedom. Any disharmony between utopia and reality exists only because of the enemies of the movement.

3. Totalitarian elements of radical Islamism

The axiomatic basic premise is – similarly, *mutatis mutandis*, as in other religions – the truth of Qur'an and hadith. The freedom of interpretation depends on the branch of Islam to which you belong. For Salafists and Wahhabis, respectively for instance Qutb and Al Qaeda – they should be taken as literally as possible. This kind of literalness has a totalitarian form that eliminates any spontaneous thinking (and capacity for it), and failure to comply against this literal interpretation amounts to apostasy which is punishable by death (Suurland 2009, 304). This totalitarian interpretation is supposed to give causal explanation of everything: of the past, present and future. Freedom to act and to ensure plurality is hindrance of the realisation of law of nature/history and of eschatology. Purification of the religion of Allah and supremacy of Islam will nevertheless happen because this is the will of Allah. This idea is comparable to the secularist totalitarian idea of the law of nature or law of history. This journey to the end is delayed by those who don't submit to Islam. Such understanding of Islam automatically creates a class of existential enemies. They stand between the state of disorder and the eschatological vision of the world perfection. According to radical Islamists to this class of enemies belong all unbelievers. To the pair ideology & terror, corresponds in radical Islam the pair doctrine of loyalty and enmity & offensive jihad.[5] The (institute of) jihad has also three dimensions of a permanent war: 1. Even if the non-believers were totally peaceful, the doctrine of enmity and loyalty would still claim that they are enemies. 2. Islam must free all people from oppression and falsehoods. The mission of Muslims is not limited by time and space but it is rather permanent (because of its universal goal). 3. If where Islam ruled with absolute authority the utopia would fail, there should be found or rather invented those who are responsible for the failure. Any failure of the system demands new enemies. A non-realization of utopia (which is highly probable) implies permanent war with mankind and reality itself. By the radical Islamic movements we can therefore observe the link between ideology and terror which individuates totalitarian movements.

---

[5] For the offensive interpretation of *jihad* see Faraj 2011. Faraj defends the account that the basic topic of Qur'an and hadith is war. He claims that we must interpret the term *jihad* literally and not allegorically. The duty which was deeply neglected is according to him jihad. This duty calls for "fighting, which means confrontation and blood". Anybody who doesn't live according to the Islamic law can be a target of jihad. Among them are not just the apostates and unjust rulers inside the Muslim community but also the enemies outside it. Majority of Muslims are convicted that Islam preaches peace and that *jihad* refers to the fight against the evil inside the soul of an individual. The real fight is justified only in case that one is attacked. Faraj disagrees. He argues against the interpretation that *jihad* is meant metaphorically and only defensively, that the violent passages in Qur'an are followed by the demands for forgiveness and mercy, and that we should distinguish between Medinian passages (revelation in time of conflicts) and the Meccan ones that stress and defend more peaceful relationships. (Juergensmeyer & Margo (eds) 2011, editorial introduction to Faraj, 62). He argues that fighting is now a duty upon all Muslims (Faraj 2011, 67) and denies that the different aspects of jihad (against one's own soul, against the Devil, and against infidels and hypocrites) are successive phases of jihad (ibid. 68). For the opposite, peaceful interpretation of Qur'an see Jawdat Sa'īd (2002).

How will these RI movements behave? Will they be "successful"? The success of these movements depends a lot on their success to persuade the ummah itself that their authority is really derived from Allah and Muhammad themselves (Suurland 2009, 306). So they will be primarily directed to the proximate enemy[6]. Under the greatest threat is therefore the Muslim world (or ummah) itself. In general, these movements will take the path like the past totalitarian (secular) movements: utopia will not be fabricated; the identification and the elimination of enemies and permanent war, respectively will take place. It seems that this terror will increase as ISIS demonstrates. They will also try to agitate and destabilize the non-Muslim societies because this causes hate, intolerance, animosity etc. what in a sense proves the doctrine of enmity and loyalty. The course of present events seems to prove this contention.

Beside common elements and similarities, we may notice also some differences or specific features of the Islamist totalitarianism: 1. unlike the secular totalitarianism, the Islamist totalitarianism seems to be without a leader (Suurland 2009, 306ff). There are certain figures or "spokespersons" respectively (Wahhab, Qutb, Zawahiri, bin Laden, Faraj) but they do not have the amount of control like Lenin, Stalin, Hitler … 2. There is no special central »official« territory or organization from which they operate and recruit their followers. Maybe ISIS is an exception. We deal with de-centralised networks and dissemination of information spread worldwide. They include dawah supported by the big Saudi and Gulf money (Ibid). 3. They are fundamentalist and in this sense retrograde and anti-modernist (they are unlike Communism which is pro-modernist), but on the other hand they share with Communism the "ethical" nature (as

---

[6] Faraj (2011, 64) distinguishes between proximate and distal enemy and claims that jihad should primarily be directed to the first, i.e. to the enemies in the Muslim world. He gave three reasons: 1. To combat the proximate enemy is more important than the fight against the distal one; 2. In the struggle against the distal enemy Muslims are/will be killed in vane; 3. The basis of imperialism in the Muslim countries are exactly the home infidels i.e. proximate enemies. The Muslim victims will be in vain if Muslims do not first set them free of their own, home infidel rulers. The fight against foreign imperialist makes sense only if it takes place under the truly Islamic flag and truly Islamic leaders. Therefore Muslims must first put in order their own house and only then and on such basis try to spread Islam as far as possible all over the world.

opposed to "aesthetical" which is characteristic for Nazism).[7] 4. Contrary to the usual fact that perpetrators of genocidal acts try to hide their crimes[8], they display their crimes worldwide. This is surely connected with their need to destabilize the (non-Muslim) world, to spread fear, panics, animosity and other negative feelings, what is of course also the feature and aim of terrorism in general. So they combine terrorism and genocide.[9] But on the other hand we may interpret this feature also in the

---

[7] Here the terms *aesthetical* and *ethical* should be understood in the Kierkegaardian sense. An illuminative Kierkegaardian interpretation of Nazism and Stalinism was given by American Christian theologian Charles K. Bellinger. According to it, Nazism is an extreme pathological example of the aesthetical "stage" (again in the Kierkegaardian sense of the term *stage* (Kierkegaard distinguished between three life "stages" or dimensions of life: aesthetical, ethical and religious)) and anxiety before the good, and Stalinism an extreme pathological example of the ethical stage and anxiety before the evil. The common denominator of both personality profiles (Nazi and Stalinist) is that the person refuses to become a self or a single individual (in Kierkegaardian sense) what means that she/he refuses the call of God to become an image of God. Such pathological personality can try to avoid his/her becoming a self in the aesthetical and ethical way, respectively. The Nazis tried to avoid the call of God and to become the self (Christianity) by trying to return to or to re-establish some form of pre-Christian (premodern) past and thus to hide themselves before God. The problem with the ethically pathological personalities is that they are pharisaic in the sense that they refuse that they are just the members of the sinful human race, and try to eliminate all sinful individuals. So they want to create an ethically ideal, ethically "pure" world without sinful individuals. They are – contrary to aesthetes (Nazis) – directed to the future, they are pro-modernist and refuse the "dirty old world" and its tradition(s). See Bellinger 1992 and 2001; Žalec 2014 and also 2015 (39–47).

[8] "There is no universally accepted definition of terrorism, but there is some wide consensus about its characteristics. Terrorism has social and political aims. The goal of unpredictable terroristic violence is to undermine the norms of behaviour, laws and ways of fighting, to frighten, destabilise, dehumanise, humiliate, demoralise etc. There are always three parts involved in terroristic attacks: attackers, victims of the attacks, and the third party for which the attacks are meant in order to frighten, destabilise etc. it (cf. Schmemann 2003)" (Žalec 2013, 67).

[9] Genocide is an inherent part of any totalitarian regime (see Žalec 2013, 68–69). By comparing the genocides (committed by totalitarian regimes or movements in the past, before the present RI (or maybe we should say before the techno-age (in the Flusser's sense of the term) developed enough) and terrorism we could say:

light of the ideas and theory, respectively of Vilém Flusser (1920-1991). According to Flusser the aim of all events, including political, already is and will be more and more, to be recorded, saved and displayed by technical images (Ger. *technische Bilder*, hereafter TIs).[10] The Islamic totalitarianism – for instance ISIS and its posting of the video shoots of the executions by decapitations of infidels can be interpreted as an evidence for this hypothesis.[11] 5. The last difference between the secular totalitari-

---

"In the case of genocides, there is no such third party [see n. 6 above – n. B.Ž.]. Quite to the contrary, in fact: public knowledge about genocides is not desired; perpetrators of genocides want to keep their deeds secret. Perhaps the best example demonstrating this thesis is Cambodia under the Khmer Rouge. First, they banished all the strangers and closed the country, almost hermetically. Then the genocide could start, and indeed it did start, taking dimensions and forms which are almost beyond imaginable" (Žalec 2013, 67). Rwanda, Turkey (genocides of Armenians), mass killings after the World War II in Yugoslavia, Darfur etc. provide additional evidence for this thesis. (Op. cit., 67 (n. 15)) But the modern RI movements or organizations (like ISIS) are counterexamples to it.

[10] According to Flusser, current events (in the techno-age) do not flow any more toward some kind of future, but rather toward TIs (photography, film, TV, video, computer graphics and images …). TIs are not windows but rather "history obstructions" (Flusser 2011, loc. 766). The goal of political demonstrations is not to change the world, but to be depicted by TIs. The same is true for the goal of battles, wars, revolution etc. Flusser stressed that the war in Lebanon was an important event, a turning point, by which we could observe the reversal of the history away from the future, toward TIs. This initiates a new kind of interaction, a feedback between the image and event. Another, concrete example to which he pointed is the TV broadcast of the fall of the Nicolae Ceaușescu and his dictatorship in 1989 in Romania. Today and in the techno-age, respectively events dine on images and images dine on events. We think that it is safe to talk about a *sui generis* mutual symbiotic parasitical participation between events and images. This is true as for the world events – for instance the landing on the moon -, as for more local, smaller events, for instance a common marriage: the integral part of a marriage is that the pair and the wedding guests get their picture(s) taken, and the wedding program adapts to photoshoot (or nowadays more and more also to recording by video-camera) (Flusser 2011, loc. 766–71).

[11] Another important aim of such displaying of the killings might be disclosed in the light of the thought of Jean Baudrillard. The danger comes from the "fact" – to which Baudrillard pointed – that today no event can avoid simulation (Baudrillard 1993). As Paul Hegarty (2004, 102) densely expressed Baudrillard's point by the example of holocaust: "Non-deniers [of holocaust – n. B.Ž.] need

anism(s) and radical Islamism – which we stress – is based on the belief of Muslims that the end of the history is in Allah's hands. Therefore in the case of RI there is no concrete image according to which we could measure the progress (of the revolution). The eschatology of Islam puts the »end of history« firmly in the hands of Allah and it can't be made immanent by man. But on the other hand there still exists also the earthly Eschaton which can be made immanent. This is the situation in which Islam absolutely rules on the Earth and in which all religion is purified for Allah. Thus we come back to the permanency of jihad and the argument for it, respectively which is based on the need to solve the problem generated by the plurality and spontaneity of human beings and in the possibility of unbelief which they imply. (Suurland 2009, 303–304)

4. Conclusion

Of course, our stance to RI should be pragmatic, but on the other hand we shouldn't cultivate any illusions about the possibility of true dialogue, appeasement, sincere cooperation, peace and peaceful co-existence, tolerance etc. with it. RI is a war against spontaneity and thus against the nature of humanity. Nothing can stop or persuade them to stop waging this war. The stronger will be their influence the stronger will be the tension between the West and the Islamic world.[12] But we shouldn't only refuse RI and fight against it, but also try to decrease the origins and positive factors of RI: it is not only poverty that we should mention as one of

---

also to be aware that to commemorate the mass murder of millions of Jews is also a dimension of it, as it transforms what occurred into hyperreal, mediatized 'reality', reducing the real event, which at the same time, replaying it, re-enacting it, to some extent (referring specifically to *Shoah*, and *Holocaust*, in *Transparency of Evil*, p. 91; 97: the book's title echoes Hannah Arendt's *Eichmann in Jerusalem: A Report on the Banality of Evil*). The denial of the Holocaust is bizarre, because there is so much proof of it occurring (even though Auschwitz itself has largely had to be rebuilt), so for Baudrillard, this is perhaps the most important thing to watch out for: it is not the absence of proof, or 'moral relativism' that lets the Nazis back in. Today the excess of truth, the hyperrealization of everything, means that no event, however momentous and violent, can elude simulation. This is the danger" (*Transparency*, pp. 91–3; 97–9).

[12] The last sentence must be understood with some reservation because Islam is a part of the West despite the fact that it has always been its other. It is safe to say that for Islamophobic persons Islam is not just other, but the Other.

them, but also crisis of identity, feelings of resentment toward the West and alienation from it (Western Muslims) etc. A thorough and exhausting consideration of the origins of RI certainly surpasses the frame of this paper. There is a phenomenon, the understanding of which is very important for understanding the factors and origins of RI. This phenomenon is islamophobia. But alas – because of the lack of space in the present book – we must stop here and postpone its consideration for some other occasion.

REFERENCES

Arendt, H. 1951. *The Origins of Totalitarianism*, Orlando: Harcourt Brace & Company.

Arendt, H. 1970. *On Violence*. New York: Harvest Books.

Arendt, H. 1992. *Eichmann in Jerusalem: A Report on the Banality of Evil*. New York: Penguin Books.

Baudrillard, J. 1993. *The Transparency of Evil: Essays on Extreme Phenomena*, London: Verso (translation of *La Transparence du Mal*).

Bellinger, C. K. 1992. Toward a Kierkegaardian Understanding of Hitler, Stalin, and the Cold War. In: G. B. Connell and C. S. Evans (eds), *Foundations of Kierkegaard's Vison of Community: Religion, Ethics, and Politics in Kierkegaard.*

Bellinger, C. K. 2001. *The Genealogy of Violence: Reflection on Creation, Freedom and Evil*. New York: Oxford University Press.

Faraj, Abd al-Salam. 2011. "From the Neglected Duty". In: M. Juergensmeyer and M. Kitts (edited and with introductions by), *Princeton Readings in Religion and Violence*, Princeton and Oxford: Princeton University Press, pp. 63–68.

Flusser, V. 2011. *Into the Universe of Technical Images*. Edition Kindle.

Friedrich, C. J. and Brzezinski, Z. 1966. *Totalitarian Dictatorship and Autocracy*. New York: Praeger.

Havel, V. 1985. The Power of Powerless, in J. Keane (ed.), *The Power of Powerless: Citizens Against the State in Central Eastern Europe*, New York: M. E. Sharpe, pp. 23–96.

Hegarty, P. 2004. *Jean Baudrillard: Live Theory*. London & New York: Continuum.

Ibrahim, R. (ed.) 2007. *The Al Qaeda Reader. The Essential Texts of Osama Bin Laden's Terrorist Organization*. New York: Broadway Books.

Jawdat Sa'īd. 2002. *Non-Violence: The Basis of Settling Disputes in Islam*. Damascus (Syria); [Pittsburgh (PA)]: Dar al-Fikr.

Juergensmeyer, M. and Kitts, M. (edited and with introductions by). 2011. *Princeton Readings in Religion and Violence*, Princeton and Oxford: Princeton University Press.

Killingsworth, M. 2012. *Civil Society in Communist East. Europe: Opposition and Dissent in Totalitarian Regimes*, Colchester: ECPR Press.

Martinjak Ratej, A. 2016. Conception of power, violence and terror according to Hannah Arendt. In: J. Juhant & B. Žalec (eds), *Which Religion, What Ideology? The religious potentials for peace and violence*, Zürich: Lit Verlag, pp. 77–85.

Marx, K. & Engels, F. 2008. *Manifesto of the Communist Party*. Radford: Wilder Publications.

Roberts, J. 2014. *Lenin, Trotsky and the Theory of the Permanent Revolution*. Kindle edition.

Schmemann, S. 2003. Terorizam protiv civila [Terrorism against civilians]. In: R. Guttman & D. Reif, *Leksikon ratnih zločina: Ono što bi javnost trebala da zna* [*Crimes of War. What the Public Should Know*]. Beograd: Samizdat B92, pp. 478–9.

Suurland, D. A. J. 2009. Totalitarianism and Radical Islamic Ideologies. In: B. C. Labuschagne & R. W. Sonnenschmidt, *Religion, Politics and Law: Philosophical Reflections on the Sources of Normative Order in Society*. Leiden and Boston: Brill, pp. 257–309.

Trotsky, L. *The Permanent Revolution*. Https://www.marxists.org/archive/trotsky/1931/tpr/pr-index.htm (January 30, 2016)

Žalec, B. 2013. Genocide as social death: A comparative conceptual analysis. *Anthropological Notebooks*, 19(2), pp. 57–74. Freely accessible at: http://www.drustvo-antropologov.si/AN/PDF/2013_2/ Anthropological_Notebooks_XIX_2_Zalec.pdf (January 30, 2016)

Žalec, B. 2014. Nazism and Stalinism in the Light of Kierkegaard's Thought. *Filozofia*, 69(5), pp. 443–450. Freely accessible at: http://www.klemens.sav.sk/fiusav/doc/filozofia/2014/5/443-450.pdf (January 30, 2016)

Žalec, B. 2015. *Genocide, Totalitarianism and Multiculturalism: Perspectives in the Light of Solidary Personalism.* Zürich: Lit Verlag 2015.

LENART ŠKOF: FAITH AND HUMILITY – ON THE FUTURE OF THEOLOGY OF RELIGIONS

This essay is an attempt to rethink philosophically some usages of religion in both theological as well as interreligious contexts. In that effort I will focus on two important thinkers, one theologian – Wilfred Cantwell Smith, and one philosopher – Roberto Mangabeira Unger, both being extremely devoted to the topic of religion and/or interreligious dialogue. W.C. Smith was one of the most prolific writers on religion and theology. Being both theologian as well as religious scholar (with especially rich knowledge of Islam, Hinduism, Sikhism and Buddhism, among other religious traditions of the world), Smith proposed to use the expression "theology of religions" in our future thinking on world religions and interreligious dialogue. Unger, on the other side, is a professor of law at Harvard and pragmatist philosopher who was in his two recent books (Unger 2007 and 2014) extremely concerned with the future of our spiritual life (both personal as well as socio-political) and religion. Both thinkers thus offer us, in my opinion, the most comprehensive view on our spiritual and religious life, in the past, and in the future.

Since my philosophical background is in American pragmatism and its rich legacies in philosophy of religion, this essay will be an attempt to think our religious future within the pragmatist and thus practical method. But let me begin here with Peter Sloterdijk and his recent book *You must change your life* (Sloterdijk 2013a) In his book, Sloterdijk is primarily concerned with the future of our spiritual-religious life. He thinks that the 19th century was dedicated to (capitalist) production, 20th century to reflexivity, and that the task of 21th century will be in practising various *exercises*. Sloterdijk replaces the old paradigms of man – *homo faber* and *homo religiosus* with a new man – *homo repetitivus* or *homo artista*, a man of ethics or a new ethical subject for Sloterdijk, being capable of doing exercises and thus being able to constantly working or improving of herself. (4) This opens an important question for us – namely why is Sloterdijk so certain about the decline of *homo religiosus* and whether his new artistic (wo)man is in fact not a result of a misunderstood view of religion in his own thought. There are some indices that our observation might be justified. For this purpose I will confront Sloterdijk's thought first with W.C. Smith's and then with R.M. Unger's theory of religion.

With Smith I intend to argue for a future theology of religions being able to secure a peaceful coexistence among world religions, with Unger I wish to enlarge or enrich Smith's argument with the ethico-political spirit of American pragmatism as found in already mentioned two of Unger's most recent books on religion. In the conclusion, I will finally try to find an answer to Sloterdijk's book main dilemma about the future of religion(s).

I

W.C. Smith (1916–2000) was a Canadian theologian and one of the leading experts in the field of world religions and comparative religion. John Hick even calls him a major comparative religion scholar (Cracknell 2001, 8). Smith was born in Toronto as a son of a Presbytherian father and a Methodist mother. Smith referred to his mother as a »warm-hearted traditionalist« (3), and it was in her work that he found the inspiration for his spiritual development. He soon fell in love with Islamic culture and civilization and started his studies in Hebrew, Arabic and Near Eastern history at Toronto University. He spent few years in Lahore (at that time still in India – Smith was there between 1939–1945, before the partitioning of India) and among his closest friends were Muslims, Sikhs and Hindus. After his return to Canada, he taught Islamics in McGill university and in 1964 he was appointed Professor of Comparative Religion at Harvard University. It is perhaps worth mentioning how his innovation in the study of religion have had important practical consequences. This is how K. Cracknell has put it in his "Introductory Essay" on his thought:

> Among his innovations at Harvard was the insistence that examiners for Harvard doctorates should be drawn from the traditions being studied as well as from the student's own tradition. As he always insisted, people mattered more than systems. One of his students at this time once remarked: 'Before I met Wilfred I studied Buddhism as a system. What I learned from him was to look for the faith of Buddhists as persons' (9).

This observation, or better, hermeneutical credo of his thought and life, devoted to religious studies, nicely captures the practical spirit of Smith's work, or, better, the *ethos* of his theory. I will now try to outline his innovative concept of a theology of religions which is perhaps the most important innovation of his work.

In his work *The Faith of Other Man* (first published in 1963), later republished as *Patterns of Faith Around the World* (1998), Smith deals with the problem of religious exclusivism and this topic will be in the forefront of my analyzes in this first part of my essay. The concluding essay of this book ("The Church in a Religiously Plural World") will be here my point of departure. In today's world of consumerism, including many so called *fast-food* religions, it is not so easy to capture the spirit of Smith's important intervention, bearing important consequences not only for interreligious dialogue but also for our ethical lives. Here I wish to introduce the first of both virtues from the title of this essay – humility. It is my firm conviction, that – once we have decided to live ethical lives within any of world religions, we have also decided to respect other ethical subjects, notwithstanding their religious faith. Here ethical intersubjectivity goes hand in hand with the ethical spirit of interreligiosity. This is what Smith means when he discusses a story, which took place at Harvard when an eminent theologian Paul Tillich was teaching there. Namely, one of his students has published a letter in a student paper, showing various inconsistencies in Tillich's understanding of Asian religions. For Smith this is now of a key importance: in our today's world, knowing other traditions is a prerequisite for any theologian. Being among the last of the so called religious isolationists, Tillich probably could not be aware yet of this fallacy. But this isolationist and exclusivist position, which today is generally unacceptable within the religious studies and most of the forms of contemporary theological thinking, is essentially linked to our ethical awareness: it is humility that must govern our theological and religious understanding. What is humility then? Let us look first at Smith's argument to be able to discuss humility from a theologically-ethical point of view:

> If Christians take seriously the revelation of God in Christ – if we really mean what we say when we affirm that his life, and his death on the cross, and his final triumph out of the very midst of self-sacrifice, embody the ultimate truth and power and glory of the universe – then two kinds of consequences follow, two orders of inference. On the moral level, there follows an imperative towards reconciliation, unity, harmony, and fellowship. At this level, all humanity is included: we strive to break down barriers, to bridge gulfs; we recognize all people everywhere as neighbors, as friends, as loved of God as we are. (...) [T]here is another level, the intel-

> lectual, the order of ideas. (...) At this level the doctrines that most Christians have traditionally derived have tended to affirm a Christian exclusivism, a separation between those who believe and those who do not, a division of humanity into a »we« and a »they«, a gulf between Christendom and the rest of the world; a gulf profound, ultimate, cosmic (Smith 1998, 134).

This testimony is what I think is the most important feature of interreligious dialogue today. Traditionally, theologians and believers (men and women of faith) have tended to distinguish both levels: we are ethical beings, we know that there are other individuals who possess and live their own faiths, and live their ethical lives, but it is *our* faith that always makes us stronger and better, or more exculusivist in the search for truth. For Smith this is arrogant and it is in a direct contradiction with the Christian ethos: it is thus "*ipso facto* un-Christian" (135). It is in this sense that Smith polemicizes with the phrase, which was under discussion some years ago in the United Church of Canada: »Without the particular knowledge of God in Jesus Christ, men do not really know God at all« (135). That is a very strong exclusivist phrase indeed. This phrase could be directly linked to the recent book by American theologian John D. Caputo, where this prominent Catholic theologian understands the very essence of our faith in the main question of the book – "What do I love when I love my God?" (Caputo, 2001, 3). But it is Lessing's *Nathan the Wise* that for the first time captures this question. In a well-known third act (scene seven) of this play, Natan and Saladin discuss the most fundamental question of religious tolerance: "What do I love when I love my God?" means that we actually have to ask ourselves the following difficult, but in fact very simple question, which I would like to propose here: "When I love my God, do I love also those, who love other God than mine?" The famous dialogue goes as follows:

> NATHAN.
> *Sultan,*
> *I am a Jew.*
>
> SALADIN.
> *And I a Mussulman:*
> *The Christian stands between us. Of these three*
> *Religions only one came be the true.*

(...)
NATHAN.
In days of yore, there dwelt in east a man
Who from a valued hand received a ring
Of endless worth: the stone of it an opal,
That shot an ever-changing tint: moreover,
It had the hidden virtue him to render
Of God and man beloved, who in this view,
And this persuasion, wore it. Was it strange
The eastern man ne'er drew it off his finger,
And studiously provided to secure it
For ever to his house. Thus—He bequeathed it;
First, to the most beloved of his sons,
Ordained that he again should leave the ring
To the most dear among his children—and
That without heeding birth, the favourite son,
In virtue of the ring alone, should always
Remain the lord o' th' house—You hear me, Sultan?
(...)
From son to son,
At length this ring descended to a father,
Who had three sons, alike obedient to him;
Whom therefore he could not but love alike.
At times seemed this, now that, at times the third,
(Accordingly as each apart received
The overflowings of his heart) most worthy
To heir the ring, which with good-natured weakness
He privately to each in turn had promised.
This went on for a while. But death approached,
And the good father grew embarrassed. So
To disappoint two sons, who trust his promise,
He could not bear. What's to be done. He sends
In secret to a jeweller, of whom,
Upon the model of the real ring,
He might bespeak two others, and commanded
To spare nor cost nor pains to make them like,
Quite like the true one. This the artist managed.
The rings were brought, and e'en the father's eye

Could not distinguish which had been the model.
Quite overjoyed he summons all his sons,
Takes leave of each apart, on each bestows
His blessing and his ring, and dies—Thou hearest me?

SALADIN.
I hear, I hear, come finish with thy tale;
Is it soon ended?

NATHAN.
It is ended, Sultan,
For all that follows may be guessed of course.
Scarce is the father dead, each with his ring
Appears, and claims to be the lord o' th' house.
Comes question, strife, complaint—all to no end;
For the true ring could no more be distinguished
Than now can—the true faith.
(...)
Let each believe his own the real ring.
'Tis possible the father chose no longer
To tolerate the one ring's tyranny;
And certainly, as he much loved you all,
And loved you all alike, it could not please him
By favouring one to be of two the oppressor.
Let each feel honoured by this free affection.
Unwarped of prejudice; let each endeavour
To vie with both his brothers in displaying
The virtue of his ring; assist its might
With gentleness, benevolence, forbearance,
With inward resignation to the godhead,
And if the virtues of the ring continue
To show themselves among your children's children,
After a thousand thousand years, appear
Before this judgment-seat—a greater one

Than I shall sit upon it, and decide.
So spake the modest judge.[1]

Sloterdijk, in his book on three monotheisms titled *God's Zeal* (Sloterdijk, 2009), sees Nathan's play from 1779 as the most important testimony of the Enlightenment in the field of religion. Sloterdijk argues that this parable is "the Enlightenment's equivalent of the Sermon on the Mount" (123) and that his interpretation of religion already precedes modern concepts of religion within the post-Enlightenment secular cultures.

It is the first sense, which is close to the Sermon on the Mount, that I also wish to bring to the fore in my reading (the second one will be visible in my reading of Unger's *The Future of Religion* in the second section of this essay). For me, the above passage from Lessing's poem *Nathan the Wise* essentially talks about humility. Towards the end of this scene, the judge (in Nathan's words) declares that in *thousand years a greater one will appear* and judge them, who are now in vain quarrelling about the authenticity of their rings. The decision, first, will take place in the future. This reminds me both of American pragmatism's orientation towards the future,[2] and of Caputo's theology of perhaps (Caputo, 2013), which, in a clear Derridaean manner, is oriented towards a future event (*avenir*) of God: with this gesture, Caputo is "signing on to the futural, to becoming" (12), where his name for the God – »God perhaps« will *insist* as the name of hope. Importantly, for Caputo, only this kind of a futural and humble talk leads to nonviolence, because, according to him, »this lack of the 'perhaps' actually can lead to violence« (161). Thus, in *thousand years, a greater one will appear*, and judge us, but now, in our present time, we will try to remain ignorant (*docta ignorantia*), humble, and patient. Such theology of humility and patience cannot cause interreligious hostilities, or any kind of violence, stemming from one's religious faith. But humility

---

[1] For *Nathan the Wise* I use: http://www.gutenberg.org/files/3820/3820-h/3820-h.htm (accesed 11/11/2015).

[2] For example, I think of John Dewey and his *A Common Faith* (Dewey 1971) where God is depicted as an »*active* relation between ideal and actual« (51). For Dewey, the meaning of our faith to God lies in our imagination and our imaginative ability to think of new, better, more just and more compassionate relations among human beings. More on this in my *Pragmatist Variations on Ethical and Intercultural Life* (Škof, 2012).

as a virtue of our relation to God is always already a part of our intersubjective relations. In a beautiful essay of another Catholic thinker, namely Jean-Louis Chrétien, a theologian Norman Wirzba reflects on humility in one of his passages as follows – and this will soon lead us to R.M. Unger's theory of religion as closely related to faith as translated into our social ethics:

> The humble person is one, who has grasped the »nothingness« of solitary life. There is no life apart from relation, apart from our mutual participation in the life of each other. This is why humble people do not try to stand out from others. They realize that an appropriate human life is one dedicated to serving others (Benson and Wirzba 2010, 249).

The *nothingness* of solitary life, as depicted in this passage, means that our egotistic and narcissistic behaviour is precisely what causes our arrogant responses towards others, including persons of different faiths or religions. In arrogance we might have company, and being arrogant we might find many followers and even wage wars with them, but in truth we are only doing an exercise of the solitary man, in all his nothingness. Here I already hint at Sloterdijk and the problem of his method: as a philosopher he affirms that what we need are exercises, which he takes from the spirit of Nietzsche's *Thus Spoke Zarathustra* and its overman (Nietzsche 2006). But Sloterdijk's fallacy is in forgetting a practical ethical demand and instead speaking of the imperative: "You must change your life!" – this imperative is problematic precisely in a way that defines our goal – from ourselves, our ascetic practices, our future anthropotechnics – as *techne*. It is precisely here that my thought diverges from Sloterdijk's: intersubjectivity, humility and faith just *cannot* serve as another bodily or spiritual technique. Tine Hribar captures the essence of this error of Sloterdijk when he rightly points to the need to understand Nietzsche as one, being open towards the future and towards the overman, and, this is the most important observation of Hribar's essay, also as a person that postulates *love* as the highest virtue of this new man (in: Sloterdijk 2013b, 690). Nietzsche captures the spirit of this in *Ecce homo* (Nietzsche 2007). The subtitle of Nietzsche's work is precisely "How To Become What You Are". But I have to wait with my conclusions; I intend now to test my argument against the backdrop of Roberto Mangabeira Unger's *The Religion of the Future*.

II

This brings us to my second example in this essay – the philosophy of religion of Roberto Mangabeira Unger. For Smith the aim of new theology of comparative religion (this is just another name for his concept of theology of religions) was the following – I will cite it in full to be able to discuss it in the light of Unger's theory of religion:

> The theology of comparative religion, accordingly, must be the product of thinkers who see, who feel, and indeed, who know men and women of all religious groups and all centuries, as members of one community, one in which they themselves participate (Cracknell 2001, 216).

How would that be possible? How can we imagine a future theology of religions? What kind of religion does it require?

Analogous to Smith's concept of humility in Unger we have vulnerability. There are three virtues of divinization in Unger, mirroring three classical Christian virtues – faith, hope and charity or love. Faith is related to our "acceptance of the vulnerability", charity to "openness to the other person", and hope to our "openness to the new" (Unger 2014, 383). The third is a typical pragmatist virtue. If we only focus on vulnerability – for Erin Gilson in her comprehensive book on vulnerability (Gilson 2014), we have always already been vulnerable, and it is our basic vulnerability that "compels or motivates ethical action" (16) and thus transforms our vulnerability into an ethical norm. But Unger goes further: for him, vulnerability is nothing less than an equivalent to faith. Our vulnerability basically is all that we have – it is from us as mortal and vulnerable beings that we act towards others (as discussed earlier with humility as basically an intersubjective relation) – with vulnerability we have to accept more risks for ourselves, and thus become more vulnerable. It is also that from our most intimate vulnerability we search for God: as mortals we cannot stand by ourselves but have to look for, as Unger as a pragmatist would say, larger life. This is the core of Unger's concept of divinization and also a first precondition for the religion of the future. Vulnerability as a virtue thus searches within ourselves for our bigger 'self', and enlarges it back towards others. Divinization thus *is* faith: our faith that with "more engagement, more connection, more risk, more vulnerability" (Unger 2014, 384) we are moving towards *life* – now of a community. This structure can now lead towards the other two virtues of Unger's religion of the future – openness to the other and openness to the new. Openness to the other (with charity, love, and compassion) has to operate among equals. It is our ability to love and care for the others. It compels us towards a future world where our divinized selves will shape a new – patient and nonviolent – if we may add, culture of love. Openness to the new now means that, in a genuine pragmatist and experimentalist manner, we always unsettle and modify our present contexts of life: we wish to live greater lives, both ethically and socially, and we want to know that there is more in us that we are willing to admit. Here religion translates into political theology – in its many ethical and social usages.

In the conclusion I would now like to reflect on vulnerability as compared to my earlier thoughts on humility. We have seen that for any religious individual it is of the greatest importance to understand the meaning of humility as a virtue for the future theology of religions. I have already pointed out that for Sloterdijk the future of religion lies in various exercises, and – in relation to the spirit of Nietzsche's *Ecce Homo* it is our task to find out who we *are*. But what does Nietzsche's subtitle "How To Become What You Are" really propose? I am inclined to say that the weakness of Sloterdijk's exercises is that they do not sufficiently relate to the intersubjective (Wirzba) or relational character of our b/Being. They are related to various techniques of our Self (even in its more or less negating, such as in various forms of mysticism). But humility as vulnerability, on the other hand, is closer to faith and grace than to any kind of (even practical) knowledge of Self and its exercises. It is closer to what Unger understands with faith – which always is "the acceptance of an enhanced vulnerability", needed for any kind of the so called »higher forms of cooperation« (Unger 2014, 371). Grace now means that this knowledge *cannot* be conditioned or activated by any of our conscious (being theoretical or practical) activities or procedures, or techniques of the Self. This is Sloterdijk's main weakness or fallacy, in my opinion. To become what we are, now translated into the theological language, points to our most intimate ontological relationality to the other, which is again – in its essence – related to our body and its ethical anatomy.[3] We can

[3] I reflected on this extensively in my *Breath of Proximity: Intersubjectivity, Ethics and Peace* (Dordrecht: Springer, 2015). With *ethical anatomy* I am thinking of the power of our sense organs and our body as a whole to first accept our

only accept others (our companions and friends in any community as a form of a cooperation) as basically vulnerable, when we finally understand, that in an intimate sense of our *daimon* (Sloterdijk would also refer to Heraclitus, but in a different way) we are secretly directed towards becoming what we always were: we thus have anthropotechnology in Sloterdijk, as a new form of Nietzsche's will to power on one, and new "ethos of being" (*daimon* according to Hribar; in: Sloterdijk 2013b, 699), which evades this fallacy and directs us towards our inner Being – with faith, understood as humility and vulnerability. Hribar thus rightly concludes on Sloterdijk:

> His immunological man is not an "ethical man" of ethos, as he would like to affirm, but an immoral man, a man beyond "good" and "evil", beyond "truth" and "lie", beyond sacrality and profanity; and it is precisely for this reason that he is blind for the sacred as sacred, for the being as being (699f.).

To conclude: being humble means to say farewell to arrogance – not only in our personal lives, but especially in the lives of our religious communities – parochially as well as globally.

REFERENCES

Benson, B.E. and Wirzba, N. 2010. *Words of Life*. New York: Fordham University Press.

Caputo, J.D. 2001. *On Religion*. London: Routledge.

Caputo, J.D. 2013. *The Insistence of God: A Theology of Perhaps*. Bloomington and Indianapolis: Indiana University Press.

Cracknell, K. (ed.). 2001. *Wilfred Cantwell Smith: A Reader*. Oxford: Oneworld.

Lessing, G.E. 1893. *Nathan the Wise*. Tr. W. Taylor. London, Paris and Melbourne: Cassell & Company Limited. (http://www.gutenberg.org/files/3820/3820-h/3820-h.htm)

Dewey, J. 1971. *A Common Faith*. New Haven and London: Yale University Press.

---

own vulnerability, only being able to translate it into an ethical awareness within an intersubjective logic based on compassion and care for others as vulnerable.

Gilson, E. 2014. *The Ethics of Vulnerability: A Feminist Analysis of Social Life and Practice.*
New York and London: Routledge.

Nietzsche, F. 2007. *Ecce homo*. Tr. by. D. Large. Oxford: Oxford University Press.

Nietzsche, F. 2006. *Thus Spoke Zarathustra*. Tr. by A. del Caro. Cambridge: Cambridge University Press.

Sloterdijk, P. 2009. *God's zeal: the battle of the three monotheisms*. Tr. W. Hoban. Cambridge, MA: Polity.

Sloterdijk, P. 2013a. *You must change your life.* Cambridge: Polity.

Sloterdijk, P. 2013b. *Spremeniti moraš svoje življenje*. Tr. by A. Leskovec. Ljubljana: Slovenska matica (with the afterword of Tine Hribar).

Smith, W.R.. 1998. *Patterns of Faith Around the World*. Oxford: Oneworld.

Škof, L. 2012. *Pragmatist Variations on Ethical and Intercultural Life.* Lanham: Lexington Books.

Škof, L. 2015. *Breath of Proximity: Intersubjectivity, Ethics and Peace.* Dordrecht: Springer, 2015.

Unger, R. M. 2007. *The Self Awakened.* Cambridge, Mass.: Harvard University Press.

Unger, R. M. 2014. *The Religion of the Future.* Cambridge, Mass.: Harvard University Press.

BRANKO KLUN: METAPHYSICS, VIOLENCE, AND VATTIMO'S POSTMODERN DEMOCRACY

We live in a time in which the term "metaphysics" has been beset with negative connotations. As a result, metaphysical thinking, in its ambition to understand the whole of reality (traditionally called Being) and to find reality's principles (in the sense of fundaments and grounds), is often associated with totalitarian pretensions. The whole is accused of being an all-encompassing totality which subjugates its parts and does not tolerate any difference or otherness, while the search for its "fundaments" is directly linked to a "fundamentalist" attitude and a violent reductionism. If we transpose this manner of thinking to the social realm, metaphysics becomes a threat to pluralistic society, which must ensure the peaceful coexistence of differing world-views. Any totalising view with one single truth thereby represents a potential danger and possible source of violence to such a society. From this perspective, we can see that the "deconstructing" or "weakening" of any strong metaphysical claim is necessary, or even imperative, as such claims could endanger the pluralistic nature of a democratic society.

In this paper, which mainly deals with Gianni Vattimo's hermeneutical and political thought, I will first provide a reconstruction of his critique of metaphysics which was largely inspired by Heidegger. Here, metaphysics is interpreted as a way of thinking which is intrinsically linked to violence, and Vattimo also recognises the remnants of metaphysical violence in the prevailing political system of liberal democracy. His critique of liberal democracy and his ideal of a hermeneutic democracy will be presented in the second part of the article. The conclusion consists of some critical reflections on Vattimo's position, and urges for a rehabilitation of the notion of truth, as well as for a more positive interpretation of metaphysics.

Vattimo's Critique of Metaphysics

One of Derrida's important early essays was titled "Violence and Metaphysics" (Derrida 1980), and Vattimo's concluding article in the book honouring his seventieth birthday is titled "Metaphysics and Violence" (Vattimo 2007). For both philosophers the connection between metaphysics and violence represents a central issue in their thinking. However, this interpretation of metaphysics cannot be adequately understood without Heidegger, who took over Dilthey's expression of the "surpassing of metaphysics" (Dilthey 1990, 126), and developed an interpretation of metaphysics as a particular "way of thinking" (Heidegger 1994, 74) which determines and dominates the history of Western philosophy. It is not the contents ("entities", *Seiendes*) of the metaphysical tradition which are at the forefront of his criticism, but rather a deeper horizon of this way of thinking or understanding of Being (*Sein*). Metaphysics takes for granted that to (truly) "be" implies stability and an immutable presence; it looks for firm grounds in a reality marked by instability and temporal change. The metaphysical quest is rooted in the human striving for a meaning which would overcome the radical insecurity and temporal finitude of human existence. For Heidegger, here lies the core of violence in metaphysics: the suppression of time (in all its dimensions) in order to assure a time-less presence, which can then be mastered and disposed of. The original sin of metaphysics therefore lies in an attitude which does not accept the historical (temporal) determination of being (and its finitude), but rather seeks to reach beyond it – to a realm of transcendent and eternal meaning. For Heidegger, the true motive of the metaphysical quest is "the will to power", which seeks to master and dominate, and this reveals the violent nature of metaphysics (Heidegger 1957, 66).

Heidegger introduced the term "Destruktion" precisely to unmask the violent acts which lie behind metaphysical notions, and to trace them back (a *re-duction*) to the horizon of temporality, within which they were originally constituted (Heidegger 1986, 39). Similarly, Derrida's *deconstruction* intends to expose seemingly stable and secure metaphysical concepts (identities) as results of violent reductions, which suppress the "other" and the original event of *differance* (Derrida 1972, 6). It is important to see that this criticism of metaphysics does not relate primarily to metaphysical questions (an understanding of the whole, looking for universal principles and grounds), but to the metaphysical way of thinking, and to its presumed motives (of power and domination).

Vattimo adopts Heidegger's criticism of metaphysics and combines it with Nietzsche's thought. These are the two thinkers "on whom he has based all his philosophical research" (Vattimo 2007, 400). Vattimo thereby developed his own philosophical position, which puts forward hermeneutics as an antipole to metaphysics. For Vattimo, similarly to Heidegger's broader understanding of metaphysics as a way of thinking and as a historical epoch, hermeneutics too is not merely a philosophical discipline, but a way of thinking which, in this case, is characteristic of our present time. Our age can be called *post-modern* precisely because of the importance of hermeneutics, which brought about the "end of modernity" by proclaiming the interpretative nature of all knowledge (Vattimo 1991, 12). One of Nietzsche's most quoted sentences in Vattimo's work is "there are no facts, only interpretations" (Vattimo 2002, 53). While modernity is still based on the metaphysical ideals of a unique rationality and of objective truth, hermeneutics stands for a way of thinking which does not allow for any stable being, any "objective presence", which would impose its truth on the recipient. Metaphysical being as something "out there", independent from human understanding, is just a specific interpretation, and one which has dominated the history of Western metaphysics. On the contrary, being is none other than an "event" (of interpretation) in human understanding. Vattimo believes this is what Gadamer's sentence, "Being that can be understood is language" (Gadamer 1990, 478), ultimately seeks to express. This leads to a critique of any ontology which would refer to an objective reality, and also of every form of realism.

For Vattimo the dissolution of the metaphysical Being is an event of emancipation, and the postmodern "transvaluation of metaphysical values" has had a profound ethical and political meaning. Metaphysical truth has all the attributes of power, authority, and domination. It demands subordination and exercises violence over the freedom and plurality of interpretations. Against this background, we can understand the positive meaning of notions such as "nihilism" (a dissolution of a presumed stability of being as well as of objective truth), or "weakening" (of strong and violent metaphysical concepts). However, Vattimo also stresses that a hermeneutic nihilism is opposed "to any current of negative nihilism" in the sense of "desperation" (Vattimo 2004, xxvi). The nihilist weakening of the existing structures of power makes room for the *pars construens*, in the sense of creating new projects and interpretations, on an individual as well as a social level.

The hermeneutic task of liberation and emancipation has been radicalised within the development of Vattimo's thinking. While in his early writing Vattimo insists on the need to "weaken" truth claims, and refers to Heidegger's *aletheia* as a way out of the metaphysical notion of truth (Vattimo 1991, 63), in his book on hermeneutic communism he seeks to do away with truth as such, as truth is equated with violence: "Violence is the political meaning of truth, because truth always implies a concluding restriction" (Vattimo and Zabala 2011, 18). Here we come very close to Nietzsche's understanding of truth, wherein truth serves the will to power. In fact, only "the strong determine truth, because they are the only ones that have the tools to know, practice, and impose it" (Vattimo and Zabala 2011, 12). Truth stands for an interpretation which has usurped power, and the holder of this interpretation seeks to exercise this power over other people. For this reason, Vattimo advocates the reversal of Aristotle's famous sentence: "Amicus Plato, magis amica veritas." Friendship, in the sense of respect for the irreducible otherness of the other person, is far more important than a commitment to truth which is – knowingly or not – an instrument of power and oppression.

This criticism of truth has been extended to any descriptive philosophy which would presume to describe reality and to reflect its truth. Since there are no facts, no interpretation can lay claim to the position of truth. The presumed neutrality and objectivity of philosophical realism is, according to Vattimo, a violent imposition of a fixed order, and its aim is to ensure stability and resist alternative interpretations. Vattimo speaks about the conservative nature of realism, and it is not by chance that the term *conservative* also has a political meaning. Here, realism is the basis of what Vattimo calls "metaphysically framed democracy" (Vattimo and Zabala 2011, 16). It is a political order within contemporary Western societies, which – although they call themselves liberal (democracies) – still adhere to metaphysical thinking and resist the deconstructive challenge of hermeneutics.

Vattimo's Critique of a Framed Democracy

Vattimo develops his own political philosophy, which understands itself as a promotion of the hermeneutical ideal of emancipation against the metaphysical rigidity of the prevailing liberal democracy. It is called *framed*, because it tends to impose a frame, a fixed order of society, and is interested in its conservation. The term "frame" – linked to Heidegger's *Gestell* (Heidegger 1994, 23) – connotes the stability of a given order; one which resists change and does not tolerate alternatives. Framed democracy is conservative: it seeks to conserve the existing liberal order and distribution of power, and presents itself as the only rational and realistic order of society. However, for Vattimo this rationality and realism are based on assumptions from metaphysics – just as capitalist economics, which forms the basis of society, tends to reveal its own "metaphysical nature" (Vattimo and Zabala 2011, 59). Liberal democracy only feigns freedom and liberty, even in the case of free elections. Vattimo writes: "Instead of systems rising through democratic elections, democracy is framed within our own liberal system, which imposes elections" (Vattimo and Zabala 2011, 57). It is therefore necessary for Vattimo to unmask this metaphysical democracy as "a system sustained by those who find themselves at ease within its order of facts, norms, and institutions. These are the winners, those who dominate within framed democracy's conservative moralized order" (Vattimo and Zabala 2011, 37-38). The existing democratic system is not a rational necessity, but a hermeneutic possibility. It is nothing but an interpretation imposed by those who benefit from this system; those who are strong and powerful in society. In opposition are the weak, oppressed, and marginalised. Vattimo's "weak thought" produces direct political implications. It is "the thought of the weak, certainly not of the dominating classes, who have always worked to conserve and leave unquestioned the established order of the world" (Vattimo and Zabala 2011, 96). It becomes clear that this established order calls for change and the liberation of the oppressed. Thus the way to Vattimo's hermeneutic communism is paved, and this communism is none other than a genuine hermeneutic democracy which has to distance itself from the remains of metaphysics, something which still determine various Marxist visions of society.

Hermeneutic democracy is the very opposite of a framed democracy. It rejects every metaphysical claim and allows a plurality of interpretations. Truth as such must be left out, discarded, or cancelled (Vattimo 2011). Vattimo writes, provocatively, "the end of truth is the beginning of democracy" (Vattimo and Zabala 2011, 23). Hermeneutic democracy offers a public space for the encounter of different interpretations beyond the hierarchies of power, precisely because there is no description of truth which would function as a metaphysical reference; there is a constant and creative production of interpretations by the members of society. Furthermore, the interactions among various interpretations take place through conversation. Vattimo rejects the notion of dialogue, because dialogue still operates within the notions of logos, order, and truth. Its aim is to conserve truth and to silence the interlocutor (Vattimo and Zabala 2011, 25). In contrast to this dialogue, contaminated by metaphysics, a conversation presupposes a creative encounter of interpretations wherein any new interpretations resulting from the conversation do not contain metaphysical claims to absoluteness and truth. "In this politics of interpretation, conversation becomes the realm where the powerful describers of the world can listen to the request of the weak and perhaps change their selfish priorities" (Vattimo and Zabala 2011, 107).

Vattimo's hermeneutics seeks to be more radical than the critical theory of the Frankfurt School, and he distances himself from the political views of both Habermas and Apel (Vattimo and Zabala 2011, 76). The communicative rationality of Habermas is based on the metaphysical ideal of reason, meaning it should also be weakened. Vattimo also criticises the leftist, social-democratic parties in Western democracies because of their compromises with the existing liberal system. Instead, he is attracted by communism, and develops his own interpretation of a weakened or hermeneutic communism. Here, we can observe an interesting shift within the development of Vattimo's thought from his weak interpretation of Christianity (with two major works, Vattimo 1996 and 2002) to a new alliance between weak thought and communism. According to him, hermeneutics carries "the possibility of renovating the potential of communism in our world" (Vattimo and Zabala 2011, 109). Just as it was with his kenotic reading of Christianity, so is communism purified of all its metaphysical elements. What is left is the vocation of the weak to challenge the established and unjust order of capitalist society. The goal of weak communism is identical to that of hermeneutic democracy. The communist "promise of a society 'without classes' must be interpreted as 'without dominion', that is, once again, without an imposed unique truth and compulsory orthodoxy" (Vattimo and Zabala 2011, 116). Weak communism does not merely remain a messianic ideal, as Vattimo believes that there are concrete and paradigmatic examples of what he calls "the communist democracies" in some South American countries, referring in his book to the leftist leaders in Venezuela (Chavez), Brazil (Lula), and Bolivia (Morales).

The Criticism of Vattimo's Postmodern Position

One may remain perplexed by Vattimo's identification of his social ideal (of weak thought and the radical plurality of interpretations) with certain leftist governments which were far from immune to violence and latent metaphysics. Can Chavism, with its strong interpretation of reality and its socialist truth, be regarded as an accomplishment of hermeneutic democracy? That aside, in this concluding reflection I do not wish to discuss Vattimo's political agenda, but rather the theoretical assumptions of his weak thought. My argument is that Vattimo establishes an extremely violent interpretation of (the whole of) reality by not being able to distinguish between the different levels of the phenomena he is dealing with. Even if he advocates the principle of non-violence – which, according to him, is identical with love as *caritas* and cannot be weakened – he himself exercises violence through his simplification and reduction.

Admittedly, in the political realm there is a prejudice towards metaphysics as a fundamentalist and intolerant way of thinking. However, the crucial question concerns how we interpret and understand metaphysics. Vattimo accepts Heidegger's criticism and similarly accuses metaphysics of the will to power and domination. Metaphysics is rooted in a particular existential disposition which, in the midst of the uncertainty and contingency of the human condition, looks for firm ground and security. According to Vattimo, we should accept our existential insecurity and understand it in a positive sense, as a radical freedom of self-projecting and self-interpreting. We have "to live without legitimizations and grounding values, that is, within antifoundationalism" (Vattimo and Zabala 2011, 98). For this, we must acquire "a particular anarchic existential disposition" (Vattimo and Zabala 2011, 100) as the counterpart to the metaphysical existential disposition. What if metaphysics is not primarily motivated by the search for security and power, but by a desire to go beyond one's own self and to attain a transcendence which cannot be subdued to one's own freedom? The metaphysical quest of transcendence can also be ethically interpreted as transcending the self-centredness of the subject. Instead of connecting metaphysics with domination and violence, we can regard it as an ethical renunciation of the self in favour of the transcendent other – figuring precisely as a limit of one's own power and domination. The history of philosophy gives more arguments for such an interpretation of metaphysics than that which Vattimo takes from Nietzsche and Heidegger. Why should the anarchic existential disposition be ethically more appropriate than an attitude of desire for transcendence?

The same can be said for Vattimo's dismissal of truth. He is right in observing that there is a connection between truth and metaphysics, or better said, between truth and transcendence. If truth does not seek to merely be an interpretation, it must in some sense transcend one's own interpretative freedom. It must be experienced as a limit of this freedom. Umberto Eco's criticism of Vattimo's position follows this line of argument and points out that "the open multiplicity of our interpretations is always confronted with the solidity of the *already given* and the *already said.* Our freedom plays on this limit" (Eco 2007, 55). Not only is the imperative of love (towards another person) experienced as a limit, but Being and language (*logos*) reveal themselves as limits to our interpretations as well. Similarly, we can interpret realism in a completely different light than Vattimo. Philosophical realism understands itself as an openness to the "things" (Latin: res) "out there" which transcend our projections and interpretations. To acknowledge the authority of the things (in) themselves does not imply – as Vattimo suggests – an attitude of domination, but rather an attitude of humility. The same attitude of humility can be found in the belief that there is a universal rationality, or a universal *logos*. Kant's categorical imperative and Habermas' communicative rationality both presuppose this kind of transcendence (of reason) which is beyond subjective (qua egoistic) freedom and interpretation. Habermas would consider his philosophical and political project as post-metaphysical, but this does not make an impression on Vattimo. Realism, Habermas, Eco – for Vattimo they all are exponents of metaphysics. How can such an interpretation not be considered violent?

Jean Grondin has provided the most thorough criticism of Vattimo's theoretical stance and of his anti-metaphysical interpretation of hermeneutics. Grondin rejects the view that hermeneutics must have deconstructive or nihilist (in the sense of Vattimo) consequences and he shows how the three main topics of Gadamer's philosophy – truth, historicism, and language – cannot be interpreted in a nihilist and relativist way (Grondin 2010). In other words, Grondin pleads for a metaphysical interpretation of hermeneutics, which respects and responds to the "sense of things" (*sens des choses* – Grondin 2013) and to the "understandability of Being". The plurality of interpretations does not have to abandon the notion of truth, and metaphysics does not have to be denounced as violent. In his *Introduction to Metaphysics*, Grondin wonders "whether the deconstruction of metaphysics is not unwittingly metaphysical. It is so since its method is archaeological and its finality is ethical" (Grondin 2012, 242).

These altered theoretical presuppositions lead to various political implications. There is no need to equate metaphysics with violence and consider it as a threat to democratic society. One could even argue the opposite. If we gave up the belief in a truth which transcends the interpretative freedom of the members of a political community, what would be the criterion for favouring one interpretation over another? Which interpretation, among many, should be taken as basis for a concrete political decision? Is not such a postmodern democracy much more susceptible to violence and arbitrariness than a society which has a "metaphysical" belief in a common and transcendent *logos* and is committed to a patient *dia-logos*? Vattimo's plea for a hermeneutic communism, which he considers "a regulative and inspiring principle" (Vattimo and Zabala 2011, 117), and his sympathies for South American leftist leaders, can have a sobering effect on his vision of hermeneutic democracy, especially when – like in recent elections in Venezuela (6 December, 2015) – people seem to prefer an oppressing framed democracy.

REFERENCES

Derrida, J. 1972: *Marges de la philosophie*. Paris: Les éditions de minuit.

Derrida, J. 1980: Violence and Metaphysics. In: *Writing and Difference*, Chicago: Chicago University Press, pp. 79–153.

Dilthey, W. 1990: *Einleitung in die Geisteswissenschaften*. Göttingen: Vandenhoeck & Ruprecht (9th edition).

Eco, U. 2007: Weak Thought and the Limits of Interpretation. In: S. Zabala (ed), *Weakening Philosophy. Essays in Honor of Gianni Vattimo*, Montreal: McGill-Queen's University Press, pp. 37–56.

Gadamer, H.-G. 1990: *Wahrheit und Methode*. Gesammelte Werke 1. Tübingen: Mohr Siebeck.

Grondin, J. 2010: Nihilistic or Metaphysical Consequences of Hermeneutics? In: J. Malpas and S. Zabala (eds), *Consequences of Hermeneutics. Fifty Years After Gadamer's Truth and Method*, Evanston (IL): Northwestern University Press, pp. 190–201.

Grondin, J. 2012: *Introduction to Metaphysics*. New York: Columbia University Press.

Grondin, J. 2013: *Du sens des choses. L'idée de la métaphysique*. Paris: Presses Universitaires de France.

Heidegger, M. 1957. Die onto-theo-logische Verfassung der Metaphysik. In: *Identität und Differenz*, Pfullingen: Neske, pp. 31–67.

Heidegger, M. 1986: *Sein und Zeit*. Tübingen: Niemeyer (16th edition).

Heidegger, M. 1994: *Vorträge und Aufsätze*, Stuttgart: Neske (7th edition).

Vattimo, G. 1991. *The End of Modernity*. Baltimore: The John Hopkins University Press.

Vattimo, G. 1996. *Credere di credere*. Milano: Garzanti. (English translation: *Belief*. Stanford: Stanford University Press 1999)

Vattimo, G. 2002. *Dopo la cristianità: Per un cristianesimo non religioso*. Milano: Garzanti. (English translation: *After Christianity*. New York: Columbia University Press 2002).

Vattimo, G. 2004: *Nihilism and Emancipation: Ethics, Politics and Law*. New York: Columbia University Press.

Vattimo, G. 2007: Metaphysics and Violence. In: S. Zabala (ed), *Weakening Philosophy. Essays in Honor of Gianni Vattimo*, Montreal: McGill-Queen's University Press, pp. 400–421.

Vattimo, G. and S. Zabala. 2011: *Hermeneutic Communism. From Heidegger to Marx*. New York: Columbia University Press.

Vattimo, G. 2011: *Farewell to Truth*. New York: Columbia University Press.

SANDRA LEHMANN: OVERCOMING THE WILL-TO-POWER. JOHN MILBANK'S DISCUSSION OF ONTOLOGICAL VIOLENCE

One of the interesting and thought provoking aspects of John Milbank's Radical Orthodox theological project is that it does not – as it is currently all too frequently the case – portray religion as a genuine source of violence but rather the so-called "project of modernity," at least in its present secular form. As Milbank shows there is nihilist violence intrinsic to secular modernity, and if religion turns violent in our days, this is so because it is affected by secular modern violence. Intellectually secular modern violence is revealed (yet not overcome) by post-modern thought while in practice it becomes especially apparent in neo-liberal economics. To quote from the second edition of Milbank's "Theology and Social Theory" that will also be the reference point of this article: "'Theology and Social Theory' was written in the middle of the Thatcherite era, out of the conviction that a theological vision alone could challenge the emerging hegemony of neo-liberalism" (Milbank 2006, XI). I think that this impulse of Milbank is vitally important, even if – as we shall see – I do not agree with the overall structure of his thought.

In the first part of this article, I will develop the main feature of Milbank's project that culminates in the opposing pair of the "ontology of violence" and the "ontology of peace." In the second part, I will show that this double ontology is not only ontologically unconvincing and politically problematic but, in fact, reveals an unintentional Nietzschean residue in Milbank's thought. In a short final section, I will propose a different ontological approach that is in accordance with the basic intention of Milbank's vision. Yet methodologically it is far more materialist in drawing, unlike Milbank, not on narratives but rather on the experience of suffering.

I. From Nietzsche to the double ontology of violence and peace

To borrow a prominent formula of "Theology and Social Theory," one may understand Milbank's Radical-Orthodox theological project to be essentially a "*Counter*-Nietzschean" project and this in the double-sense that, first, Milbank develops a decisive alternative to the Nietzschean understanding (actually the understanding *à la manière de* Nietzsche) of being and the human condition as well as in the sense that, secondly, in counter-acting the Nietzschean perspective, Milbank's project remains related to it and even entangled with it. Accordingly, Milbank himself states that "the relation of ["Theology and Social Theory," S.L.] to Nietzsche is pivotal" (Milbank 2006, XIX). This positive reference to Nietzsche has to do with the fact that for Milbank Nietzsche summarizes the main characteristics of the modern episteme. One could say in a sense with Nietzsche modernity is coming into its own. This coming-into-its-own, however, has not the character of an ultimate fulfilment. Rather it is the exposure of tendencies which are essential for modernity even if, for quite some time, they remained concealed.

First, Nietzsche shows that the claim of neutrality that goes along with universal, enlightened reason is presumptuous. In fact, there is no superior formal authority of truth. Rather, reason or more precisely what reason claims to be true, is always already involved in processes of interest as well as in processes of power that go beyond reason or are, in a constitutive sense, prior to reason.

Second, Nietzsche shows that as a result of the primacy of power processes our understanding of the world primarily is not formed by rational insight but rather by myth, that is, by specific ways of interpretation or narration that, again, go beyond reason and are prior to it. Summarizing the above, one may say that the insight of Nietzsche which is dear to Milbank is the ultimate nihilist character of modern pure reason: pure reason cannot ground itself. In fact it rests on the abyss of power processes. It is nothing beyond these power processes, and it can only escape the nihilism which threatens to undermine it, if it explicitly faces this problem.

Both Nietzsche's exposure of the alleged neutrality of reason and the actual primacy of myth Milbank uses in order to pursue the proclaimed interest of "Theology and Social Theory," namely, to show that the claim of secular social theory to exhibit the social meaning and function of religion in a scientifically neutral way is unfounded; that rather the secular understanding of religion is part of a wider mythic self-conception inherent to the modern episteme.

Milbank goes beyond Nietzsche, however, in developing an independent genealogy of "the myth of secular social theory." First he shows that modernity draws on a neo-pagan element that consists in a Macchiavellian approach to political thought since the Renaissance. More importantly, the secular episteme is derived from heterodox developments in Christian theology during the Late Middle Ages, namely, both a secularized voluntarism and a providentialism (cf. Milbank 2006, 9–47). Milbank uses this insight in order to reject the claims of contemporary theory of religion to give a coherent interpretation of religious phenomena. Eventually, this theory only serves as a means of justifying the preliminaries of the modern discourse in general. Because of its truncated perspective it is unable to demonstrate the most essential aspects of religion, especially, of the Christian religion. In a decisive turn of perspective, Milbank declares theology to be the true social theory – at least, if it is radically orthodox in the way he imagines it to be, i.e., based on a both post-modern and neo-platonic understanding of classical Christian authors, above all Augustine, but also Thomas Aquinas.

Since secular social theory is anchored in the secular episteme, it is obvious that Milbank's project is much more far-reaching than the sociological focus of "Theology and Social Theory" suggests. In fact, it is because of its ontology that "Radical Orthodoxy" hints at a genuine alternative to the existing modern project, that is, at a mode of thinking and being in which modernity overcomes itself in order to fulfill what it claimed for at its beginning: a human order of freedom, justice, and solidarity.

Consequently, also the opposition that is the theoretical centerpiece of "Radical Orthodoxy" is ontological by nature. According to Milbank the theological aberrations of Late Medieval theology result in a secular "ontology of violence" that comes into its own in the Nietzschean type of thought. Its counterpart is Milbank's radically orthodox Christian "ontology of peace" that is situated in post-modernity; but that proposes a path out of it. To behold the whole panorama of this opposition, one should add that, for Milbank, the Nietzschean violent mode of thinking is the main feature of post-modern thought. In a sense, in Milbank, "Nietzscheanism" is Nietzsche plus the main line of post-modern discourse. This includes in particular Heidegger, Deleuze, Derrida, and Lyotard.

Let me briefly sketch out the main characteristics of an "ontology of violence." According to a "violent ontology," the basic character of being is neither defined by rational subjects nor by substantial objects. Rather, being consists in a continuous process of differentiation from which beings evolve according to their respective force of will, their *conatus* that always is a will to power. This process of the manifold wills to power is irreducible. There exists nothing prior to and beyond it, so that it can be conceived as an end in itself. Every individual being forms itself over against all others and, in doing so, it is a manifestation of sheer power. This means that there is no communality other than that of difference through power, the communality of a constant struggle which only knows the value of being stronger than others and overcoming them.

From my perspective, Milbank's genealogical critique of secular modernity is most convincing on the formal ontological level, i.e., where he identifies the univocal character of violent modern/post-modern ontology and, as a countermove, pleads for the reopening of an analogical ontological approach.

Ontological univocity was first thoroughly developed in the 13th century by Duns Scotus. Following him, in order to understand the recognizability of God or absolute being by finite reason, one has to assume that all concepts, irrespective of whether they are applied to finite beings or absolute being, always have the same content. This conceptual univocity also applies to the term "being" itself since, for Duns Scotus, "being" is the most general concept, i.e., even if it does not have unity of genus (*Gattungseinheit*), it is universally valid. In post-modern thought, Deleuze took ontological univocity up again and made it a key element of his philosophical opus magnum "Difference and Repetition." In fact it seems that Milbank's depiction of ontological univocity refers more to Deleuze than to Duns Scotus. Thus, Milbank claims that with univocity there is no more absolute being but only "Nietzschean" finite beings struggling for their own existence; a struggle in which they arise out of nothing as fast as they disappear again. Univocity of being, therefore, is nihilism because the One is Nihil realizing itself in a violent process of differentiation.

Milbank's alternative to univocal ontology is a renewed version of analogical thinking; "a renewed version" because Milbank integrates a post-modern differential motive and, unlike the scholastic tradition, develops an *analogia entis* detached from the Aristotelian-Thomist "pros-hen-relation." According to it, every finite being is directed toward the singular absolute substance (God) which it represents in a deficient, finite way. In contrast, in Milbank's version of ontological analogy, God is both "a superabundant Being" (Milbank 2006, 430) as well as "an internally creative power" (Milbank 2006, 430) that differentiates itself in order to "finitely 'explicate'" (Milbank 2006, 431) itself. Hence, "the created world of time participates in the God who differentiates" (Milbank 2006, 431). Every finite being is fully included into the dynamics of the absolute that manifests itself in and through finite being while at the same time pointing beyond finite being. To be in an analogical way, therefore, means that there is a vertical movement in finite being, i.e., to be is to be beyond oneself in the direction of that which brought oneself into being and, thus, forms one's very essence; an always dynamical essence, to be sure.

The prospect of the "ontology of peace" is opening up if one considers that the absolute that differentiates itself through individual finite being does so in differentiating itself through *all* finite being. This means that in striving (and realizing itself) beyond itself, each individual being always also pursues the absolute analogical dynamics of all other beings, i.e., their respective self-realization. The true meaning of difference is, therefore, to harmoniously support the difference of all other beings.

II. The violence of harmony, and the peace in suffering

Let me emphasize that, in my view, the main claim of Milbank's "ontology of peace" is seminal, that the present task of Continental Philosophy, indeed, is to develop a positive understanding of difference or the "unrest of finitude," i.e., to understand the invisible (and therefore "bottomless") ground of being in the sense of an absolute positivity that points finite beings beyond themselves, that is, beyond the finite conditions in which they appear in the "zone of visibility." Yet, as already mentioned, I disagree with the details of Milbank's theoretical framework. There are two reasons for this that are closely connected. Put briefly Milbank's ontological perspective is deficient (I) for he remains caught in the Nietzschean primacy of the will (II).

In respect of the first point (I), Milbank does not in my understanding adequately take into account the negativity of finite being; hence, his opposition between the "ontology of violence" that bears the traces of an absolute finitude and the "ontology of peace" that has always already overcome all violence is too simplistic. If applied to the social-political sphere to which Milbank's project is primarily directed, his simple ontological opposition creates a dichotomy that is obviously problematic, namely, a dichotomy between violent secularism, on the one hand, and peaceful radical orthodox theology, on the other. Obviously, this is a troublesome continuation of Augustine's doctrine of the two cities, of earthly *imperium* and the heavenly *ecclesia* (cf. Milbank 2006, XVI). Lest I be misunderstood, Milbank knows very well that there is a violence in being that also affects religious practice whenever it gets involved into politics. Thus, concerning the necessary "imperial," i.e., political connotations of religious practice, he states: "(…) insofar as *imperium* lies outside *ecclesia*, it is an essentially tragic reality, involved in a disciplining of sin, which threatens to be itself nearer to the essence of sin (than the sin punished; S.L.)" (Milbank 2006, 425). Yet, Milbank's ontology of peace leaves no room for this insight. Instead, he evokes the guiding principle of "fraternity through harmonious consensus" (Milbank 2006, 422) which is realized by Christianity, since Christianity that is based on an ontology of peace is "'peaceful transmission of difference'" (Milbank 2006, 422).

Milbank's discussion brings to mind the criticism of the concept of consensus in authors such as Jacques Rancière and Jan Patočka. Both show in their own way that starting with the guiding principle of harmony, there follows a practice that, in fact, petrifies the always violent status quo of a given order, i.e., a practice that accepts violence for the sake of harmony. Accordingly, following Augustine, also Milbank affirms "the need of some measures of coercion" (Milbank 2006, 424) in the social context he envisions. It makes things even worse when, in contrast to "the (purely, S.L) earthly city" (Milbank 2006, 424), coercion here has "the true final peace in view" (Milbank 2006, 424).

In contrast, I think that it is necessary to both recognize the violence of being as well as to show that it does not have the last word, i.e., that there, indeed, exists an ultimate horizon of peace. We have to accept that there is violence as for example in the shape of coercion. Yet, the recognition that there is violence is connected with the ontological obligation (i.e., an obligation in accordance with what could be called "the impetus of being") that we will always have to overcome it again. Given the conditions of finitude, peace can never be represented through order, even if it is the most harmonious one. Rather, peace manifests itself in the constant and ever new overcoming of violence.

In respect of the second point (II), the dichotomous character of Milbank's ontology obviously has to do with the fact that Milbank, against his own claim, does not overcome the Nietzscheanism that he himself criticizes. The ontology of violence and the ontology of peace, therefore, stand against each other like two wills to power for Milbank's theoretical presuppositions remain deeply rooted in the post-modern, Nietzschean scheme. What is real has no irreducible status of its own. Rather, as indicated above, Milbank follows a narratological concept. The real is *narration*, a symbolic order plus the practices implementing it. Consequently, Milbank qualifies his own discourse as a "metanarrative," or more exactly, as the "version of an Augustinian metanarrative" (Milbank 2006, XXI) that is "not entirely distinct (from, S.L) the Nietzschean metanarrative" (Milbank 2006, XXI). There cannot be a clear distinction between the two metanarratives precisely because they share the same narratological presuppositions. This results, first, in the levelling of transcendence. Like the "Nietzschean" discourse the "Augustinian" discourse of Milbank, too, does not refer to the beyond but to the narrative gesture establishing it. Secondly, there is the precedence of strategies of rhetorical and/or aesthetic overwhelming over those of intellectual rigor and transparency. Admittedly, for Milbank there is no other truth to Christianity but the power of persuasion. As Milbank states himself: "I do not think that there is any way of demonstrating [the] ontological priority of peace" (Milbank 2006, 440). Accordingly, it is a matter of willful implementation. There is only one small element of demonstration in Milbank's discussion when he refers to the fact that human desire, in general, prefers peace to violence and meaning to meaninglessness. Yet, he has to leave it open why this desire exclusively represents the "truly-desiring reason of the truly-desirable" (Milbank 2006, XVI). He can only argue this statement with his own narrative. But as we know since Plato's dialogues such as "Protagoras," "Gorgias," or the "Republic," it is far from clear what we should truly desire. Is it pleasure? Or is it justice? And as Plato also shows, we need more than rhetoric means to decide on this.

Let me finish with the short outline of an alternative concept. Methodologically, in order to meet Milbank's ontological claim, it is necessary in my view to return from the narratological to the phenomenological level where things come to show both themselves and that what does not appear. This implies that the reference point has to change. Unlike Milbank I propose to start with suffering instead of desire which as such can have any direction. In suffering there occurs a dynamic in which violence as well as the prospect of possible pacification, finitude as well as infinity overlap.

In the immediacy of suffering there emerges what is lacking and also what forms the condition of possibility for suffering, i.e., integrity, wholeness. Every suffering, while testifying to privation, also testifies to this wholeness. At the same time, in its immediacy, it demands this wholeness. Ontically and in concrete phenomenal existence this demand or claim can take different forms, for example, the claim to justice, the claim to be equally treated as human beings, but also most basically the claim that "this pain should stop." Even or, rather, precisely in the most extreme phenomenal cases, suffering and the claim to salvation implicit in it demonstrate that there exists an ontological orientation towards integrity or wholeness that is stronger than the pain tying the suffering being onto itself. However, ultimately, and acute consolation notwithstanding, this wholeness can never be fulfilled under finite conditions. To put it pointedly, our existence is always a matter of suffering and a constant experience of violence.

If philosophy focuses on this violent aspect of being alone, that is, detached from the transcendent background of wholeness, it results in the Nietzschean structure: every being strives for wholeness, and it does so against all other beings insofar as they threaten to limit its driving force. Thus, there is the necessity of violence in finite being. Yet, it is also possible to understand – in a reflective step beyond suffering – that one can only be striving for wholeness in truly being with others; that the striving for wholeness is a manner of overcoming the finite conditions of my existence which also implies overcoming myself towards the others, as for example, in acts of solidarity with those others who suffer.[1]

REFERENCES

Milbank, J. 2006: *Theology and Social Theory. Beyond Secular Reason.* Second edition. Oxford: Wiley-Blackwell.

---

[1] I would like to thank my colleague Dr. Andreas Telser, Assistant Professor at the Institute of Fundamental Theology and Dogmatics at the Catholic Private University Linz, for the illuminating discussions on Milbank in particular and on contemporary theology in general.

MARIO WINTERSTEIGER: THE BENEFICIAL POISON OF MYTHOLOGY. REFLECTIONS ON GEORGES BATAILLE'S ANTHROPOLOGY OF MYTH AND VIOLENCE

Introduction

"Man does not live by bread alone, but by poison."[1] (Bataille around 1940, cit. in N.N. 1985, 7). This one-liner by French philosopher and mythologist Georges Bataille can be seen as the guiding theme of our reflections on what we may call the beneficial poison of mythology. To be specific, our aim is to infuse some kind of poison into the discourse of political philosophy – of course not in order to harm society, but in order to help it via inoculation or immunisation. As it seems, political thought has too long been living "by bread alone", since its contemporary outlook has been shaped by abstract ethics of distribution (cf. Ankersmit 1996, 2 ff.). Issues of "bread" – like economy and social justice – are indeed essential, but they should not be the *only* topics of political philosophy; especially today, in our postmodern times, it also has to deal with the question of how we can act prudently in the face of the "return of the myth" (Bohrer 1980) and of the violent acts committed by new nationalisms and fundamentalisms. And concerning these troubling issues it seems to be more enlightening to deal with "poison" (à la Bataille) than to deal with "bread alone".

The current *mainstream* of political thought still seems to be surprisingly helpless in regard to the challenge by myth and violence; it has not drunk up its beneficial poison, because it has been all too heavily inclined towards a 'politically correct' suppression and tabooing of humankind's disagreeable sides (cf. Bohrer 2004, 9 ff.; Wiechens 1995, 93 ff.). Therefore, still it shies away all too often from the "dark" insights of political philosophy and mythology (cf. on them Wintersteiger 2013, 191 ff.). Basically, we all know the old call "Know thyself" (cit. in Neubaur 1980) since ancient Greek times. But political anthropology, which could help us in this process, has after all been almost criminally neglected by postmodern political theory (cf. Illies 2009, 196 f.). However, the problems we have mentioned cannot be solved if they are just pushed aside (cf.

[1] Throughout this essay, all translations from German sources are our own.

Wiechens 1995, 93 ff.) or if one ignores their anthropological foundations. As Bataille (1994, 9) says, “man can *overcome* what frightens him”, but only if he dares “facing it” (ibid.). Obviously, getting to know ourselves is something that cannot be accomplished by way of ‘political correctness’ and ‘fair weather philosophy’ alone.

The relevance of Georges Bataille for political thought

In which way can someone like Georges Bataille help us in this situation? Why should we refer to this unruly child of philosophy, to a man who was working on a “mythology of violence” (Bohrer 1998, 143) and who was obsessed with eroticism, Greek tragedy and the old gods (cf. on that Bischof 2010, 48 f.)? Since he does not seem to offer any really useful *practical* outline,[2] his importance for political philosophy is due to something else: Robert Pfaller (2013, 219) is absolutely right when saying that Bataille’s strength lies “in his discoveries”. We will deal with two of them that are associated with his so-called “sociology of the sacral” (Moebius 2006, 135).

Since his ideas are – in the words of André Masson – “bitter medicine and without sugar icing” (Masson 1987), Bataille is still considered a ‘politically incorrect’ thinker (cf. Finter 1992, 7). He receives comparatively little attention in the German speaking countries (cf. ibid.; Wiechens 1995, 101 f.), while the situation is slightly different in France where he has been vindicated by the postmodern turn (cf. for that ibid., 28 f.; Bischof 1984, 346 f.; Lange 1992, 108 f.). Indeed, there are some aspects that can make him look suspicious to us, for example the obscure features of his secret society *Acéphale* (cf. on them Moebius 2006, 253 ff.; Bischof 2010, 111 ff.), especially the rumours about a planned sacrifice (cf. for this ibid., 125–133) and, above all, the attempt to put myths into political service (cf. on that ibid., 9 ff.).

Those who are therefore inclined to brand Bataille as an almost “fascistic” thinker (cf. e.g. Ottmann 2012, 254) nevertheless completely misunderstand what his work is all about; it has to be considered as an essen-

---

[2] After all, his downright “intoxication of revolution” (Moebius 2009) and the corresponding political actions with *Contre-Attaque* have not been very successful (cf. ibid. 2009, 92–98); the quasi-religious experiments with *Acéphale* have not been either (cf. Bischof 2010, 111 ff.).

tially anti-totalitarian enterprise (cf. Bischof 2010, 102 ff.); first, it is about a rehabilitation of the "dark" side of political philosophy – the so-called "dark authors" in the sense of Critical Theory, e.g. a tradition that includes the Marquis de Sade and Friedrich Nietzsche (cf. Horkheimer and Adorno 2011, 126 f.), two authors much valued by Bataille (cf. Bataille 1999; Bataille 1987, 91–114); second, his work is about gaining psychological knowledge of "affective powers" (Bataille 1978, 42) within society – insights he assumed to be the foundation of the forging of effective political weapons (cf. ibid., 42 f.; Moebius 2009, 93 f.). In our reflections Bataille is less important for being a smith who is producing weapons for political discourse than for being a mythologist confronting the people with their "abysses" (Masson 1987); in doing so, he gives us a potentially beneficial poison to drink, namely a philosophy of wastefulness (cf. Bataille 1985, 7–31), of sacrifice (cf. Bataille 1997, 39 ff.), of violence and myth. Here we will only mention two disturbing but stimulating insights as a foundation for the work of political philosophy.

Insights into the fascination of myth and violence

In late 1933 and early 1934 Georges Bataille published a short study titled "The psychological structure of fascism" (Bataille 1978). It is a text in which he comes to the conclusion that the ideological "mass excitement" (ibid., 33) of his time cannot be explained in a materialist way (via economy) but only in terms of psychology (cf. ibid., 38; Bischof 2010, 64). For our topic here it is particularly interesting that Bataille interprets fascism as kind of a "return of the repressed" (Bischof 1978, 98), as something that occupies a field that had become empty (cf. Bataille 1978, 41). Of course, similar things could be said about religious 'totalitarianism' (cf. ibid., 33). Bataille claims that the primary factor for the related "psychological fascination of the masses" (Moebius 2009, 94) is the dangerous or the rejected which is assigned taboo: sadistic violence, the sublime and the sacred (cf. Bataille 1978, 16–22) are considered the most important sources of that sort of power (cf. ibid., 37). From Bataille's perspective, an ideology such as fascism could only be successful because modernist societies had abandoned emotional matters like myth almost without battle – instead of themselves satisfying the related needs of the people (cf. for this Moebius 2009, 99). This is the first of the dark insights that are important here, i.e. the first drop of Bataille's beneficial poison; following Rita Bischof (2010, 11) we could call it the "*dialectic of myth*".

Let us now turn to the second insight; it is related to the "fascination of violence" (Wiechens 1995, 92). In a collection of texts on "The Abolition of Economy" Bataille (1985, 45–48) describes "surplus energy" as a potential danger for every social system; whenever jamming occurs, it is advisable to look for "possibilities of decongestion" (ibid., 48); and if we repress this fact, we are in danger of witnessing a "catastrophic" outbreak (cf. ibid.). This was said in a primarily political and economic context, but it could also be a guideline of Bataille's "mythology of violence" (Bohrer 1998, 143). Political anthropology is generally known for assuming some human disposition for aggression (cf. Illies 2009, 201 f.). In Bataille's works we find many reflections on the problem that violence can be a fascinating thing of some sort; some examples are Bataille himself being captured by the "mentality" of Spanish bullfighting (cf. on that Mattheus 1984, 55 ff.), his thoughts on the startling photos of a "Chinese torture" that can be found in "The Tears of Eros" (cf. Bataille 1993, 246 f.), and finally his ideas on crime stories that live from being fascinated with danger and victims (cf. Bataille 1994, 85).

In the literature following Bataille, these aspects of his "mythology of violence" (Bohrer 1998, 143) are seen as evidence supporting two assumptions: First of all, a *total* "abolition of violence" is (probably) impossible (cf. Wiechens 1995, 93 ff.); secondly, a complete "taboo on violence" can be dangerous (cf. ibid.) because – according to Bataille – it seems to be the forbidden fruit that is most fascinating (cf. ibid., 94; Bataille 1994, 123 f.). Accordingly, the logical conclusion is that we must provide a somewhat rational abreaction (cf. Wiechens 1995, 94 ff.). This is the second insight, another drop of Bataille's beneficial poison.

Conclusions

Which conclusions can be drawn from these dark lessons about the irrational "border regions of human life" (Moebius 2006, 13)? What is the task of political philosophy in the face of myth and violence? It must develop social strategies that can prevent a "catastrophic overspending" (Bataille 1985, 48), in this case an uncontrolled outbreak of the most toxic and violent forms of myth. But this cannot succeed if we taboo the need for myth (cf. for this Bohrer 1980) and the fascination of violence.

The idealistic "repression of the evil" (Bohrer 2004, 14) seems to have its dangers; as Bataille writes, such a misjudgement makes us suffer helplessly from what we otherwise could self-confidently fence in (cf. Bataille 1985, 48). Reflecting on all this is the task of the social sciences and of a political philosophy that has to describe how to control the "asocial" phenomena of life (cf. Illies 2009, 195).

In his book "The Shadow of Dionysus" the sociologist Michel Maffesoli demonstrates a possible way out: In order to prevent a destructive "return of the repressed", people must pay tribute to their passions – in the sense of some sort of catharsis (cf. Maffesoli 1986, 110 f.); this has to be done in small, controlled doses – quasi "homoeopathically" (cf. ibid., 113); and this happens through rituals, festivals, games and so on (cf. ibid. 110–113). Following Bataille's lead, one could say: "If man must not act like a maniac, he must admit madness its part." (Bataille 2012, 96). The related literature speaks of a "constructive channelling or 'abreaction'" (Wiechens 1995, 96) without which the danger cannot be banned (cf. ibid., 93–96). We could also call it a small, beneficial dose of poison that immunises people. Myth and violence within culture – e.g. in literature and film (cf. on them Bohrer 1980) – must not be branded *per se*; otherwise they might return someday in another, perilous form and in a catastrophic dimension.

REFERENCES

Ankersmit, F. R. 1996. *Aesthetic Politics. Political Philosophy Beyond Fact and Value*. Stanford: Stanford University Press.

Bataille, G. 2012. *Die Aufgaben des Geistes. Gespräche und Interviews 1948–1961*. Berlin: Matthes & Seitz.

Bataille, G. 1999. *Wiedergutmachung an Nietzsche. Das Nietzsche-Memorandum und andere Texte*. Munich: Matthes & Seitz.

Bataille, G. 1997. *Theorie der Religion*. Munich: Matthes & Seitz Verlag.

Bataille, G. 1994. *Die Erotik*. Munich: Matthes & Seitz.

Bataille, G. 1993. *Die Tränen des Eros*. Munich: Matthes & Seitz Verlag.

Bataille, G. 1987. *Die Literatur und das Böse*. Munich: Matthes & Seitz.

Bataille, G. 1985. *Die Aufhebung der Ökonomie*. Munich: Matthes & Seitz.

Bataille, G. 1978. *Die psychologische Struktur des Faschismus. Die Souveränität*. Munich: Matthes & Seitz Verlag.

Bischof, R. 2010. *Tragisches Lachen. Die Geschichte von Acéphale*. Berlin: Matthes & Seitz.

Bischof, R. 1984. *Souveränität und Subversion. Georges Batailles Theorie der Moderne*. Munich: Matthes & Seitz Verlag.

Bischof, R. 1978. Über den Gesichtspunkt, von dem aus gedacht wird. In: G. Bataille, *Die psychologische Struktur des Faschismus. Die Souveränität*, Munich: Matthes & Seitz Verlag, pp. 87–120.

Bohrer, K. H. 2004. *Imaginationen des Bösen. Zur Begründung einer ästhetischen Kategorie*. Munich and Vienna: Carl Hanser Verlag.

Bohrer, K. H. 1998. *Die Grenzen des Ästhetischen*. Munich and Vienna: Carl Hanser Verlag.

Bohrer, K. H. 1980. Rückkehr des Mythos? Bemerkungen zu ein paar Motiven pessimistischer Kultur. *Frankfurter Allgemeine Zeitung*, 26.01.1980, p. 25.

Finter, H. 1992. Vorwort. In: H. Finter and G. Maag (eds.), *Bataille lesen: Die Schrift und das Unmögliche*, Munich: Wilhelm Fink Verlag, pp. 7–10.

Horkheimer, M., and Adorno, T. W. 2011. *Dialektik der Aufklärung. Philosophische Fragmente*. Frankfurt am Main: Fischer Taschenbuch Verlag.

Illies, C. 2009. Die Bedeutung von Anthropologie und Evolutionswissenschaften für die politische Philosophie. In: D. Jörke and B. Ladwig (eds.), *Politische Anthropologie. Geschichte – Gegenwart – Möglichkeiten*, Baden-Baden: Nomos, pp. 195–229.

Lange, E. 1992. „Georges Bataille échappe à l'explication". Zur Rezeption Batailles in der französischen Literaturkritik der sechziger und siebziger Jahre. In: H. Finter and G. Maag (eds.), *Bataille lesen: Die Schrift und das Unmögliche*, Munich: Wilhelm Fink Verlag, pp. 101–117.

Maffesoli, M. 1986. *Der Schatten des Dionysos. Zu einer Soziologie des Orgiasmus*. Frankfurt am Main: Syndikat.

Masson, A. 1987. Über Georges Bataille. In: *Der Pfahl. Jahrbuch aus dem Niemandsland zwischen Kunst und Wissenschaft I*, Munich: Matthes & Seitz, p. 232.

Mattheus, B. 1984. *Georges Bataille. Eine Thanatographie I*. Munich: Matthes & Seitz Verlag.

Moebius, S. 2009. Im Rausch der Revolution: Kunst und Politik bei André Masson und den surrealistischen Gruppierungen *Contre-*

Attaque und *Acéphale*. In: L. Hieber and S. Moebius (eds.), *Avantgarden und Politik. Künstlerischer Aktivismus von Dada bis zur Postmoderne*, Bielefeld: transcript, pp. 89–110.

Moebius, S. 2006. *Die Zauberlehrlinge. Soziologiegeschichte des Collège de Sociologie (1937–1939)*. Konstanz: UVK Verlagsgesellschaft.

Neubaur, C. 1980. Fest, Rausch, Opfer. Georges Bataille: „Die psychologische Struktur des Faschismus“. *Die Zeit*, 28.03.1980, p. 88.

N.N. 1985. Hinweise. In: B. Mattheus and A. Matthes (eds.), *Ich gestatte mir die Revolte*, Munich: Matthes & Seitz Verlag, pp. 7–12.

Ottmann, H. 2012. *Geschichte des politischen Denkens, Vol. 4/2: Das 20. Jahrhundert. Von der Kritischen Theorie bis zur Globalisierung*. Stuttgart and Weimar: Verlag J. B. Metzler.

Pfaller, R. 2013. *Wofür es sich zu leben lohnt. Elemente materialistischer Philosophie*. Frankfurt am Main: Fischer Taschenbuch Verlag.

Wiechens, P. 1995. *Bataille zur Einführung*. Hamburg: Junius.

Wintersteiger, M. C. 2013. The ‚Art' of Social ‚Mythmaking'. The Social Function of 'Mythic Infrastructure'. In: E. Kapferer, A. Koch and C. Sedmak (eds.), *Strengthening Intangible Infrastructures*, Newcastle upon Tyne: Cambridge Scholars Publishing, pp. 181–196.

NADJA FURLAN ŠTANTE: "POWER OVER" HIERARCHICAL DOMINATION: A STEM CELL OF VIOLENCE

Introduction

Dear ladies and gentlemen – in such frequently used addresses the special respect for women and gender equality is not in itself reflected. What such addresses do represent is at least an apparent attempt to enter the female element in the wider social and religious life. Given that we were used to reverse syntax in the past decades, which lingers somewhere in the back of our head (dear gentlemen and respected ladies ...), it is an encouraging innovation, which reminds us that the time has come when the justice is finally being done and achieved from both extremes. However, there is still a long way to achieve gender balance. The real gender equality would be achieved when the latter becomes a part of our consciousness, not only the legal basis: when feminine operating modes are recognized as equal to masculine. If humanity remains only at the level of legal equality, and not integrated into our mentality, in the collective memory, the emancipation would only be a long march through institutions. Establishing ethical humanization of human relations in the light of gender equality is, therefore, a process that began with the installation of legal basis and should continue on epistemological basis. The way of thinking is to be altered. Taking this way we are burdened and limited by a number of barriers which prevent us to achieve the ideal of harmonious coexistence of differences and interpersonal relationships.

In striving for gender-equality we should not overlook or ignore the impact of gender stereotypes and prejudices which contribute a considerable share in the preservation and creation of gender hierarchies. Their logic is the logic of domination and "power over" of one gender over the other. Because of their denotement with values, they promote the fight or the competition of strength and power between genders. With this they make us distant from the desired ideal of cooperation between genders and basic human dignity, which is the foundation of human rights. Should dignity truly be real, we need to go beyond the mere legislative level of norms and rules, we have to transfer them from paper to life, from theory to practice. And here we are, in spite of the desire for equality and gender equality, hampered by gender stereotypes and prejudices that are hidden and work under cover, as if from ambush waiting for the right moment.

The concept of power represents a fundamental challenge for many different forms of feminism, too. Early feminism, for example, recognised the distinction between "good power," which had a liberating character and freed everyone, not just women, from the shackles of confinement and oppression, and the "oppressing or enslaving power", which is seen as "bad power." The patriarchal form of establishing power – patriarchal power – is from the feministic perspective understood as bad power – with devastating consequences (Jarl 2003, 44).

Starhawk also differentiates between three kinds of power: "power over," "power within," and "power with". Power over is the basic mode of power of patriarchal societies. It expresses the logic of domination by which some, mostly elite males, dominated women and subjugated classes and races, as well as the nonhuman world. This kind of power is fundamentally competitive. The more power one side has, the less the other side has. Power within, by contrast, is a process by which dominated people shake off the control of others and their own realization of the powerlessness and inferiority projected on to them, laying hold of their own innate power and goodness. Power with is the development of ways to share power that do not negate others in order to affirm oneself, but can mutually affirm one another, while being able to acknowledge the special talents of particular people. In this relation of mutual empowerment each person flourishes by also promoting the flourishing of others (Radford Ruether 2005, 95–96).

The path leads up to the ideal of the path changes. G.K. Chesterton says that it must be the one who wants to achieve and assess your progress, strictly faithful to the ideal of change and must not start having affairs with ideals of uniformity. Because progress cannot alone make progress (Chesterton 2001, 33).

Therefore, if we are to make progress towards better mutual relations, we should primarily be aware of the harmfulness of negative gender stereotypes and prejudices and resist the inertia of maintaining the status quo in the situation that allows such prejudices and maintains it. Despite the many laws that attempt to codify equality and gender equality, our environment is in practice still a very fertile breeding ground of "traditional" images, to which women and men should get as close as possible. Hierarchical system, negative gender stereotypes and prejudices support and encourage one another. Therefore, with the desire to break the logic of domination and power we need to move forward on the path of human charity, love and compassion, which is the call of all the major religions and urges us to improve mutual relations.

This is not to change the form, but to focus is on the re-evaluation or even better, enrichment of specifics or different genders, therefore in overcoming the current hierarchical set of gender images. Male is superior, female is inferior – this denotement should be replaced with equivalent. It is necessary to emphasize that the transformation and change must be approached holistically. No human right is safe if we do not strive to protect all in the same way, no change in relation to the transformation of interpersonal relationships, prejudices and gender stereotypes could bear fruit without taking into account of their coherence and complexity.

In this context, the close link between prejudice, negative gender stereotypes and physical violence should also be noted.

Crisis in relationships and physical violence

Human's position in the world today, could be illustrated by the following metaphor by Grmič: a human’s situation in the world today could be expressed by the metaphor to say that today's humanity is positioned on a draft which occurs when all the windows and doors are open in a tidy home, and suddenly nothing stands firmly anymore and is in danger of tipping over or being blown away from home to an unknown location (Grmič 2002, 13). Considering all events and heterogeneity that characterize the situation in which we live nowadays, there is more and more violence against a single human being, of human communities and nations, and against nature which particularly threatens humanity and all of life on earth.

Self-existence, rule and self-purpose of technocratic-bureaucratic system which is placed on a hierarchical pedestal above the humanity and within which there is no room for sensitivity and compassion for others, all facilitate terrorism of all kinds and forms, which is increasingly expanding and getting worse and worse shapes. Intimidation and manipulation go hand in hand and make healthy relationships impossible and also restrict the views that may get a humanity out of this predicament; the mind gets dimmed and wrapped in fear, which in turn leads to recklessness and quick reactions. Violence is still being eliminated by violence, by force and there is no way out of the vicious circle. It seems like a humanity with all this anxiety, dissatisfaction, frustration and fear loses ethical principles and the very foundations of morality and ethics. Violence adopts various forms and activities: covert and not so covert violence has become a habit of postmodern human. Gender stereotypes and prejudices in a world where violence is a reality of everyday life draw strength from him/her and create a new, covert violence. This can result in physical forms of violence. Sexual violence is closely associated with certain cultural notions of gender differences and the related assessments and identifications of a particular gender as inferior or superior. According to Darja Zaviršek

> cliché definitions of femininity and masculinity lead to the fact that women and men in different social situations comply with them, i.e., in accordance with the expectations of the society. This division seemingly explains sexual violence and also makes apologies for it. (...) The difference that exists at the level of clichés, the man is in certain examples perceived as a beast (especially in the case of an individual from the lower social classes, for any different or ethnic groups), and in other cases he is totally exonerated from guilt (he got carried away in drunkenness, a woman has provoked, he is mentally unbalanced). On the other hand, a woman is either a helpless victim (because she is weak men should constantly protect her, supervise her, take care of her and teach her), or it is all her fault (because she provoked, because she was not responsible enough, because she made wrong choices or because she was not a good sexual partner, because she was a too present or not enough present mother). Such definitions of men and women are stereotyped and at the boundaries of morality, on top of this they are dependent on the existing ideologies. That is why the evaluation of sexual violence is not judged much by the very acts, but regarding the context in which the person who carried out the violence is placed. In other words, sexual violence will be defined as such regarding the fact where a woman and a man are located on the map of social context. (...) A woman is only a body through which power relations are manifested (Zaviršek 1996, III.–VI.).

Women as a means to achieve the objective, which is in this case a demonstration of and fight for power, are exposed to various forms of violence. At the same time gender stereotyped images and prejudices and cliché images have an important role. With its covert message that promotes the struggle for power they increase physical violence of men against women.

In some places in the former Yugoslavia a generally accepted prejudice is accepted, namely, that women like being beaten from time to time. This shows who is the boss in the house. Some social attitudes towards women can therefore inspire men to see the woman as a loot to be won, conquered or included in their property, which must be kept under control. Z. Kanduč refers to a declaration of the anthropologist Peggy Reeves Sanday who arguments the distinction between societies with few rapes and those societies where rapes happen often. Peggy Reeves Sanday notes that there is less physical violence in interpersonal relationships in the societies that are more equal and where gender relations are more symmetrical and harmonious (Kanduč 1998, 199). In this respect cultural norms that promote violence against women either rape or any other form of physical violence contribute significantly to the increase in violence of one gender over the other. There is also the myth of the monstrous male sex drive, unequal distribution of social power in favour of men and against women on the one hand, and the socialization of women in the role of victims – subordinate, inactive, dependent, accepting, patient, kind, compassionate, weak the person on the other side. Many gender stereotypes and prejudices that are arranged in the form of standards, in addition to other factors (personal trauma, alcohol intoxication, economic deprivation ...) promote physical violence and silently justify it in the background.

In relation to rape, a strongly linked myth is also the one that too often occurs among men as well as in the society as a whole. The myth *that women say no but they mean yes*. There is also the stereotype that women dress, communicate and visit certain places in order to provoke rape. *This is a shallow excuse*, says the former Head of the Criminal Section of the District Court in Celje, the judge Milko Škoberne as he further explains: "*Even if a woman walks around naked she is protected by law in her sexual integrity and nothing must happen to her or nothing should happen to her*" (*Ona*, July 20, 2004, 17).[1] That this is a myth is supported by

[1] Milko Škoberne was a determined opponent of sexual violence against women and children but, unfortunately, is also the first judge in the history of Slovenia

the fact that not only young women in short skirts are abused and raped, but also babies, girls, also boys and older women.

Harmfulness and influence of certain negative gender stereotypes and prejudices is even more acute, because the myths and shifting of blame at the expense of prejudices and stereotypes are often stimulated precisely where victims should achieve at least some justice and perpetrators should be punished for the undisputedly unacceptable and intolerable behaviour. Screaming headlines frequently reveal and remind us of the taboos of modern times. As reported by many newspapers and also appearing on the National Court there are trials supported by stereotypical thinking. N. Prah notes an example of the judge Richard Bertrand, who in 1982 commented his verdict in favour of the accused with the words that "*it is utterly reckless of any girl to hitchhike at night. That does not need to be debated. She is asking for it*" (*Ona*, July 20, 2004, 18). Similar statements can be witnessed in our courtrooms today, as usually the defendants do not deny the offense but they try to prove that sexual intercourse was consensual. "*Mainly the defenders of the offenders rely on stereotypes as they wish to denigrate the victims after proceedings have already come quite far. They suggest that women were flirting, seducing, they describe how they were dressed, they argue that a normal woman is not to be seen at such a place at such a time, etc. But regardless the story it is to be respected, if a woman says no*", explains Milko Škoberne (*Ona*, July 20, 2004, 18).

Negative gender stereotypes and prejudices at the expense of women therefore radically curtail basic human dignity. The struggle to recognize them is important, as well as striving to gradually replace them with healthy views on a fellow human being and on genders in their humanity. Head of the SOS phone programme, Dalida Horvat calls on everybody to actively participate in the identification and elimination of gender stereotypes, prejudices and myths that they maintain: "*Mentality needs to be changed, we must take violence from private into the social sphere. Namely, it has social roots and it is based on our social relations. This is where violence against women stems from, being a result of unequal distribution of family and social power between genders. It is a tradition of education, i.e. gender-specific socialization of girls and boys, as well as*

---

who is convicted by a final judgement because of bribery and abuse of authority (*Slovenske novice*, October 28, 2014).

samples that are transmitted. We have to change them because we are obliged to change them" (*Ona*, July 20, 2004, 18).

The fact that violence against women still has a very strong presence in Slovenia nowadays is also stressed by a number of NGOs. Ana Čefarin's newspaper article points out that police data recently shows that the number of criminal acts of domestic violence in Slovenia is decreasing, but the Head of the SOS phone programme Dalida Horvat warns in this regard that this does not mean that violence actually decreased. She further notes that since 2008, when the Act on Prevention of Domestic Violence was passed, much has been done in this direction, even the number of reports increased, state institutions were very active, especially the police. Frightening and interesting is also the fact that since the beginning of the economic crisis in Slovenia, especially the last two years, reports of the crimes again began to decline. According to Dalilda Horvat "*this is linked to the general situation – that in these circumstances it is easier to suffer than to risk that you have to search for an apartment on your own these days, etc. I would say that violence may be exacerbated in times of crisis because people in these frustrations resort to the ways they are familiar with. If this is violence, then they frequently use this ... We cannot say that the crisis is the cause, but it is certainly one of the factors"* (Dnevnik, November 25, 2013).

Because of violence of all forms and types, power games, struggles for power and dominance, relationships are doomed to fail. The crisis of human relationships has reached a devastating stage, as it seems in view of the intensity of the struggle for supremacy and power,. This is reflected both in interpersonal relations in the workplace and in partnerships or family relationships. Everyday relations are namely under attack of agony of power and violence. Intolerance, litanies and anger are the logical consequence of the fear of losing power. Instead of love, many relationships are marked by the struggle for (pre)dominance.

The interplay between the oppressed, oppression and fear is described by Paulo Friere. According to him, the fear of freedom is characteristic of all those who suffer from any form of marginalization or oppression. Indeed, the oppressed internalize the image that an oppressor holds about them, fear and helplessness are imprinted in the subconsciousness. The pattern of subordination thus becomes their way of functioning and operation. This remains even after the oppressor disappears, or when foreign oppression stops. In order to fully liberate the oppressed from the pattern of fear, they have to change it and replace it with the pattern of autonomy and responsibility (Friere 1993, 29). The human is in this respect placed in the position of an oppressor and a victim at the same time. Thus, when the fight for (pre)dominance occurs, so does the mechanism of oppression. Both men and women are in regard with gender stereotypes and prejudices placed in the role of an oppressor and a victim. The use and presence of bias has a disruptive impact on relations as it fosters a hierarchical distribution of power, which highlights the patriarchal and oppressive norms. In this respect, the woman is oppressed twice: firstly, by the men and the patriarchal norms of masculinity as something generic and, secondly, by gender stereotypes and prejudices which maintain such a norm.

Thus, when one understands the operation and the effects of the oppression mechanism, when one recognizes the dehumanization as a result of oppression, then they are on a better way to free themselves and also the oppressors. Freire draws attention to the contradiction between humanization and dehumanization. Both the object and the subject of oppression, namely, the oppressed and the oppressor are marked with dehumanization that results in injustice, alienation, lack of freedom, fear and ignorance. However, in his opinion, oppression and dehumanization does not constitute a sealed fate of mankind. This may be changed through critical insight and assessment. Thus, when the oppressed get free of images of oppression they liberate themselves from oppression (Friere 1993, 33). To become liberated one needs a path that humanizes, therefore, a path of nonviolence, a path of love. To help today's man/woman get free from hierarchical fighting for power over, one must first be aware that the struggle for power is a force which has a devastating impact for oneself and mutual relations. Later on one must realize or identify negative gender stereotypes and prejudices that have a devastating and destructive influence, as they enslave, restrict and oppress a human‘s liberal view of the other and, nevertheless, his/her own.

It is, therefore, a question of ethics and ethical values today. It is a question of the true humanization of humanity, for a responsible liberation of men and women from the yoke of slavery with power and domination. The enslavement of the human by the desire for power is characterized by fear that is becoming increasingly visible, when loosening the ties and mechanisms that allow the struggle for power over.

Logic of Love versus Logic of Domination

Fighting and bravery are usually associated as male features or stereotyped images of masculinity, which are often associated with violence. It is hard to imagine fighting and courage in a different sense than in the sense of fighting for (pre)dominance that can be associated with violence. However, there have been some individuals, both female and male in our century who have demonstrated that it is possible to fight and show courage without using violence. At least some of them found inspiration for a new way of demonstrating power and fighting spirit in the story of Jesus and his non-violent way of life. The idea of fighting without violence is thus deeply rooted in Jesus, the man who was nailed to the cross. Jesus, who taught people to love their enemies showed with his own example the need to lead the battle in such a way that you help your opponent discover his or her better side in the deepest sense of the word. Jesus teaches us to carry out our actions in the spirit of love and dignity. Non-violent struggle is characteristic of Jesus. Therefore, a man in the struggle for human rights and the struggle to amend and abandon the existing negative stereotypes and prejudices, should use the strategy of abandoning violence and adopting charity and love towards one's fellow human being.

The logic of domination that is characteristic of patriarchal androcentrism and follows the principle of violence, says that *it is easier to accuse one gender than excuse the other* (Beauvoir 1999, 21), is no longer acceptable for the global ethos which emphasizes the dignity of every human being. Different forms of masculinity and femininity in terms of patriarchal struggle for (pre)dominance always reflect the balance of power and the violence being carried out at the expense of the oppressed, i.e. women. The logic of love goes beyond, beyond the logic of domination. In light of the logic of charity and love negative gender stereotypes, prejudices and hierarchical struggle between the genders, as well as the competition for superiority, become absurd and highly visible so that they themselves begin to draw attention to their unfounded basis, harmfulness, lack of ethic and immorality.

The time of change and transformation is a critical time since the genders are in search of a new image and new antagonisms as well as exposed to significant negative factors and influences. It is therefore all the more important that society and religion at this time appeal to the logic of love and not domination, appeal to love, not power and violence. The logic of love emphasizes and brings together male and female gifts or diversities and does not assess them through the lenses of superiority or inferiority. It stems from the belief that the future does not belong to neither women nor men, but to cooperation between them. *Thanks to the duality of male and female humaneness is realized in full* (John Paul II 1995, 19).

Therefore, within the differences and specifics of both genders, the logic of love is first and foremost looking for humanity and the values that will, no matter whether they are male or female in the biological or social sense, eventually contribute to a better, more humane world. In particular, there is the search for the path that will allow each human being to become a better person. Therefore, one must, first of all, face the fact that he or she arises from relations, that he or she urgently needs another person and that the others are indispensable. A person without other persons cannot grow, cannot advance, even less can one measure his or her progress. By accepting one another and giving each other to another in the light of love, we strengthen and expand the love that keeps us and enriches us. By seeing others in the light of their dignity and uniqueness, the logic of domination vanishes, the same logic that supports the „give me – I give you“ relations, and we deem prejudices and gender stereotypes as unnecessary clutter that burdens our relations and places distorted images within them, images that fill us with violence.

The logic of love emphasizes that people are one tribe, one family (unity in a team or a team in unity) that should cooperate in harmony for the benefit of all its members, and goes far beyond the idea that a human is a wolf to another human. The fundamental connectedness of all people is reflected in the dignity of every individual. Pope Francis defines the dynamics of human relations in the light of the logic of love and the fundamental need for another man with the following words: "*A sense of internal cohesion with other beings cannot be genuine if the heart does not possess tenderness, compassion and care for other people*" (Francis 2015, 51).

The power of compassion and love unites and does not separate. On the path of integration, which is seen in the relation to the other man, love is the key to healthy and happy relationships and is manifested in the willingness of acceptance and tolerance towards each other.

Conclusion

The dominance of reason over emotion, the body over the spirit, a human over nature, a man over a woman, masculinity over femininity ... this struggle for a hierarchical domination of the above mentioned binaries takes place both in every individual and on the level of female-male relations, as well as on the broader social and religious level. Prejudices and stereotypes that often distort the image of human personality are contrary to the logic of compassion and love that accepts one such as he or she is, in particular, the love that allows one to be empowered and to find one's own self. A number of negative gender stereotyped images and prejudices are a product of the socio-religious influences and the games of relationship regarding the (pre)dominance between the genders. Such stereotypes are an accessory of social gender, which fades in the light of love. They are an obstacle to men and women on the path of creating a new paradise, they make both communication and mutual respect difficult. They create distorted images and labels that characterize the other person and return back to us in the form of a mirror image, therefore they mark and also define ourselves as well. The hierarchical supremacy in this segment is thus perceived as a stem cell of violence against the two genders, which needs to be replaced with the logic of love.

REFERENCES

Beauvoir, de S. 1999: *Drugi spol I.* (*The Second Sex*). Ljubljana: DELTA.

Chesterton, G., K. 2001: *Pravovernost.* (*Orthodoxy*). Celje: Mohorjeva družba.

Črnič, A. 2014: TedX Ljubljana. Govor. (*Speach*). http://new.livestream.com/zivo/TEDxLjubljana/videos/68430174 (19.11.2014)

Dnevnik, (2013): *V teh časih lažje trpeti, kot pa tvegati in oditi.* (*In these times better to suffer than to take the risk and go.*)

http://www.dnevnik.si/slovenija/dan-boja-proti-nasilju-nad-zenskami-v-teh-casih-lazje-trpeti-kot-pa-tvegati-in-oditi; (Novembre 25, 2013).

Freire, P. 1993: *Pedagogy of the Opressed.* New York: Continuum.

Grmič, V. 2002: Etika popolnega humanizma za danes. (*Ethics of complete humanism for today*). *Znamenje* 1-2, 13–22.

Janez Pavel II. (John Paul II). 1996: *Pismo ženskam vsega sveta, A ciascuna di voi* (slov. prevod: *Mednarodno leto žensk)* CD 62. Ljubljana: Družina.

Jarl, A., C. 2003: *In Justice: Women and global economics*. Minneapolis: Fortress Press.

Kanduč, Z. 1998: Spolno nasilje (posilstvo), kriminološke in kazenskopravne perspektive. (Sexual violence (rape), criminological and criminal law perspectives). *Anthropos* 30, 187–208.

Ona 2004: *Spremeniti je treba mentailteto*, (*We must change the mentality*), July 20, 2004, 17-19.

Poling, J., N. 2002: *Masculinity, Competitive Violence, and Christian Theology: The Sprirtuality of Men*. Minneapolis: Fortress Press.

Slovenske novice, 2014: *To je prvi sodnik v zgodovini Slovenije, ki je pravnomočno obsojen.* (*The first judge in the history of Slovenia who is convicted by a final judgement.*)

http://www.slovenskenovice.si/crni-scenarij/doma/je-prvi-sodnik-v-zgodovine-slovenije-ki-je-pravnomocno-obsojen (Octobre 28, 2014).

Zaviršek, D. 1996: *Od nične ozaveščenosti do nične tolerance. Spolno nasilje.* (*From zero awareness to zero tolerance. Sexual violence.*) Ljubljana: Visoka šola za socialno delo.

ROK SVETLIČ: THE COMMUNIST HYPOTHESIS AND THE SECOND VATICAN COUNCIL

The title of the symposium where this article was presented was "Religion, Violence, Ideology". In constellation of these three concepts, religion can get different roles. It can be interpreted as the trigger of violence, as the ideology *par excellence*. But we can also, on the other hand, demonstrate its potential for social reconsolidation, showing that the most basic values of coexistence are imbedded in every known religion. The approach to religion in the present paper will be, however, entirely different. Religion, more precisely, *philosophy* of religion will be used as the meta-position, as a tool that enables us to recognize, to understand, and to describe ideology and its affinity to violence.

Philosophy of Religion as an Optic

The reason that we use religion for this task is its capability to demonstrate the truth *as a truth*. Using Hegel's terminology, religion is a part of the *absolute* spirit, together with art and philosophy. Consequently, religious discourse is not about the truth of *this or that* sentence, fact, and proposition. Hegel: "*Religion is not consciousness of this or that truth in individual objects, but of absolute truth, as the truth of the Universal, the All-comprehending, outside of which there lies nothing at all*" (Hegel 1895, 22). To put it shortly, instead of analysing particular elements of ideology-discourse, we will use philosophy of religion because it enables a sight on the *totality* of the Being. It will be demonstrated that a certain ideological concept is very similar to the understanding of the Being that was characteristic for the medieval Christianity. Consequently, also the problem that accompanies the attempt to put this concept in political actuality is similar.

The subject of criticism will be the neo-Marxian ideology with its affinity to violence. We will refer mostly to two authors, A. Badiou and S. Žižek, but present analysis will be applicable also on many other authors from this provenience. We will focus on *specific* understanding of the Being that inclines the ideology to the radical distinction between the world as it is, and the idea of justice. In other words, we will put special attention to the *hostility* between the communist hypothesis and democracy. As a tool we will use, as mentioned, Hegel's philosophy of religion, especially the interpretation of religion in his lectures on philosophy of history, where a specific process is described. The starting point of this process is at first an entirely *abstract* notion in which the cognition is grasped that neither a human being nor the Absolute can be defined without each other. In religious language, this notion is described as Jesus Christ, who is interpreted by Hegel as the "hinge" of the whole world-history.

The destination of the process is, however, political and legal efficiency of this notion, its *actuality*. The most illustrative examples of this efficiency is the codification of human rights. The core of the culture of human rights is the concept of human's dignity, at first defined only by abstract characteristic as *imago Dei*. Today human's dignity is protected by concrete legal institutes, specific articles in penal codes, underpinned by the power of state. This process, to put it shortly, can be described as the journey of human's dignity from the sky to the ground.

But the journey was not smooth, the sky has resisted to arrive to the ground, to become actual within people. Good example for this resistance is the 3rd commandment (Ex 20), abbreviated in this sentence: "*Thou shalt not make unto thee any graven image*". The crucial shift represents the appearance of Protestantism. From this extremely reach phenomena, we will isolate only one aspect: with Protestantism, a certain boundary is torn down. The boundary between the holiness of specific places, persons, objects on one hand, and the rest of the world on the other. In *this* world there is no truth. The trace of the truth, of the "beyond", is isolated only on consecrated church, consecrated priest, and consecrated items. When Protestantism tears down the boundary between these realms, the whole world – i.e. the state and the law – can become spiritual: "*There is but one conception of freedom in religion and the state. This one conception is man's highest possession*" (Hegel 1895, 247).

Analogous to the elimination of the boundary just described the shift that is introduced by the Second Vatican Council can be interpreted. It is about the shift that is the most illustrative in difference of attitude to human rights of *Syllabus Errorum* and *Pacem in Terris*. To summarize: the subject of this paper is the attack on democracy and human rights, carried out by radical political philosophy. We will try to demonstrate that the same deficiency as it was characteristic for the medieval Christianity is characteristic also for these philosophical concepts: the incapability to overpass the boundary between the sky of ideality and political realm.

Boundary

In this chapter, we will describe the exclusion of the truth out of the world. In works of A. Badiou, for instance, this exclusion is present everywhere where he discusses the possibility to think the politics. He categorically rejects that democracy could grasp the political truth by its most basic instrument, by the election. "*Why the devil would 51 percent of the French be "the" French*" (Badiou 2008a, 22), exclaims Badiou. To demonstrate that the empirical collection of public opinion (i.e. the election) can never be the method to recognize the truth, he uses the example of transition from geocentrism to heliocentrism. He argues, if the "public opinion" was the reference of the truth, we would still live in the geocentric picture of the world. Precisely its disregarding has led to the truthful picture, i.e. to heliocentrism.

This argument is problematic. Philosophy has proved on different places that the *absolute* distinction between the consciousness of community on one hand and the ideal on the other, leads to aporias. Badiou does not realize that this argument is destructive for his own account of (political) truth: precisely the "public opinion" was necessary for the heliocentric perspective to become valid. Without the consciousness of the majority the truthful cognition would never become *actual*. Badiou's communist hypothesis is actually a good example of contemporary geocentrism: it is the announcement of the truth that rejects its verification by facts and by the thinking of citizens as well.

To put it shortly, the crucial message of radical political philosophy is the following: never, at any cost we may say "yes" to the world. Neither to democracy, neither to public opinion, neither to any other experience of life. This is the attitude of radical political philosophy toward the realm on *this* side of the boundary. Beyond it, however, the "true" truth is hypostased and its fragile description is known as the communist hypothesis. This "beyond" sometime strikes on the world as the lightening does. This phenomenon Badiou describes as the *event*. In the first place, the event is not a fact, something massive and present. On contrary, it is that what is "lacking" to the fact. Through the event, the truth is present in the absent way: "*For barley has the event appeared then it has disappeared. It is no more than a flash of supplementation. Its empirical character is that of an eclipse*" (Badiou 2008a, 123).

The event can be parallelized with the Catholic concept of the miracle. This is a mystery way in which the hint of radical “beyond” is present “here”. But this contact of two worlds triggers no interaction. The “truth” strikes on the world but remains totally separated, like a drop of oil on the water. But the goal is achieved: even if the event is not real – i.e. it is not a fact – it is still *more* than nothing. It is a tiny hint or a trace that enables the insistence on the plausibility of the communist hypothesis.

The trace of the beyond on this world is not produced only by the event. Badiou talks also about “holy” persons – about priests in some sense – that also represent the trace of the truth. These are immigrants, especially illegal immigrants. S. Žižek, similarly, argues that only the subject who is totally excluded from the (immoral) truth of the world can incarnate the truth of another world. In this sense, immigrants are the inheritors of the symbolic status which proletarians in the classical Marxism have had. Therefore, illegal immigrants are blessing for the repugnant capitalism world: they offer us an opportunity for redemption from being white “civilised” provincials. Badiou: “*Let foreigners teach us at least to become foreign to ourselves, to project ourselves sufficiently out of ourselves to no longer be captive to this long Western and white history has come to an end, and from which nothing more can be expected than sterility and war. Against this catastrophic and nihilistic expectation of a security state, let us greet the foreignness of tomorrow*” (Badiou 2008a, 70). The same idea is reflected, for instance, also in Hart-Negri concept of “multitudes”.

Violence

Frank affinity to violence is the most disturbing part of the contemporary radical political philosophy. It is important to consider that the reference on violence is not introduced on *a posteriori* manner, as the response on an extraordinary incident when conflicts or antagonism could not be reconcilable by any other means. As demonstrated in the previous chapter, the boundary between two realms is *eo ipso* statement about the *irreconcilable* conflict between them. If democratic culture insists on the ideal of the reconcilability of antagonisms – using Kant’s words, on the perpetual peace – this attitude for the communist hypothesis is the treachery of the truth. That is the reason why the most severe attacks on democracy and human rights are focused precisely on their pacifism-ideal.

Violence is a negation. The negation of smothering that already exists. If the conflict between the "beyond" and "here" is dogmatically presupposed, the ceasefire of conflicts would mean nothing but a philosophical surrender, the abandoning of the commitment to the truth. In Badiou's view, democracy has degraded man to an abject existential status when "*the only thing that can really happen to someone is death*" (Badiou 2001a, 35). Sanctity of life – the core of human rights – is nothing but the vicitimological definition of a human being. The democratic ideal that there is no need to die for something is a nihilistic sign that there we have lost the sense to live for anything.

As mentioned, violence is not *a posteriori* a part of ethical living – as a necessary coercive element for the protection of human rights –, it is *a priori* a component of a radical criticisms of democracy and human rights: "*We must examine the revolutionary work as a homogeneous multiplicity wherein terror functions as an inseparable category, and specifically as one that is inseparable from virtue*" (Badiou 2001b, 138). The same disregard to pacifism is typical also for Žižek's philosophy: "*There is nothing ethically more disgusting than revolutionary Beautiful Souls*" (Žižek 2009, 5). It is impossible to support the idea of radical equality and to insist on life as a supreme value. On contrary, persistence on democracy and peace is nothing but the treachery of the truth.

Summary

We started this article by mentioning two different strategies that can be employed to carry out the criticism on radical political philosophy. We could take particular premises and demonstrate their deficiency, inconsistency or even contradiction hidden in them. In some extend we have indicated that approach at Badiou's reference on geocentrism. In this paper, however, we have used another strategy. As a tool, we used philosophy of religion, thinking that offers a universal optic on the totality of the Being. Religion is the screen of the spirit and makes possible to grasp the self-understanding of a certain age.

Hegel's philosophy of religion demonstrates the defects of the medieval Christianity, its incapability to overpass the boundary between realm of the truth beyond and the political reality. The same characteristic can be recognized at radical political philosophy, especially at its criticism on democracy and human rights. At this point, the solution can also be suggested in the language of philosophy of religion: the communist hypothesis will become an advantageous part of the contemporary political thinking only if radical political philosophy will be capable to carry out something like the Second Vatican council. A fundamental and honest reconsolidation with the world.

REFERENCES

Badiou, A. 2008a. *The Meaning of Sarkozy*. London: Verso.

Badiou, A. 2008b. *Conditions*. London/New York: Continuum.

Badiou, A. 2001a. *Ethics*. London/New York: Verso.

Badiou, A. 2001b. *Metapolitics*. London/New York: Verso.

Hegel, G. W. F. 1895. *Lectures on the Philosophy of Religion*. London: Kegan Paul, Trench, Truebner & co.

Hegel:, G. W. F. 1986. *Vorlesungen über die Philosophie der Geschichte*. Frankfurt am Main: Suhrkamp.

Žižek, S. 2009. *Parallax View*. Cambridge/London: MIT Press.

VOJKO STRAHOVNIK: RELIGION, GLOBAL JUSTICE AND HOSPITALITY

Global and cosmopolitan justice

The concepts of global justice and cosmopolitan justice both figure within an exceedingly broad area of global ethics. The development of the area of global ethics and its justification are first and foremost grounded in a response to the recognition that the gravest moral challenges that we are facing today, are global in their essence and can only be answered within a similarly global framework (Singer 2004; Audi 2007; Sen 2009; Appiah 2007; van Hooft 2009). Some authors are even employing the conception of planetary ethics in relation to these (Benhabib 2011, 193). Thus, the task of global ethics is, first and foremost, to scale ethical dimensions of such a condition and put forward normative frameworks of global or transnational justice, collective action, maintenance of peace and set the limits of an acceptable and productive division of moral labour.

Global justice is an aspect of global ethics, that is centred on justice on a world scale, focusing especially on the domain of international and global institutions and those actions and policies of states and other actors in the global sphere that affect the world order (Nagel 2005, 113). Within such a perspective, it searches for the universal standards of justice. It can be divided into two parts, the first one encompassing political dimensions of justice and the second part encompassing socio-economical dimensions of justice. The former focuses on the just processes of (global) governance, justice as an aspect political decision making and protection of basic human rights, while the latter encompasses a plethora of issues and questions related to social, economic and cultural statuses and conditions, including aspects of poverty and inequalities, distribution and exploitation of resources, global rules of trade and the possibility to access the global markets, etc.

Cosmopolitan justice can be defined as a view within global justice, or a conception of global justice, that starts from the presupposition that "every human being has a global stature as the ultimate unit of moral concern" (Pogge 2002, 169) and is, in this sense, individualistic and inclusive (Beitz 2005, 17). It is individualistic in a sense that it gives priority to individuals as a basic moral unit of global justice, as opposed to states, peoples, or other groups when considering a global justice framework. Thus, the international sphere of justice is not seen merely as a society of states or peoples arriving at rules of mutual recognition and conduct, and limiting justification within these groups. Cosmopolitan justice is based upon the presupposition, which demands that justice "derives from an equal concern, or a duty of fairness, that we owe in principle to all our fellow human beings, and the institutions to which standards of justice can be applied are instruments for the fulfillment of that duty" (Nagel 2005, 119). At the same time, the position of cosmopolitan justice is inclusive in that it does not leave out any individual or group based on whatever criteria it might be offered for such a special case.

While we have seen an increase of interest in global ethics, it is important to note that global ethics for the globalized world requires several important changes of perspective when considering global justice. One of the changes pertains to who is to be considered as an agent of such justice and how we can delimit the scope of its responsibilities and corresponding obligations; any "viable theory of justice for the contemporary world ought to have some way of coming to grips with the changing centres of influence and advantage that make our world very different from the world of free republican states envisaged in Kant's Perpetual Peace" (Nussbaum 2006b, 324.) This also includes the incentive to search for centres of influence and power beyond national states as bearers of responsibility in regard to global justice and determining their corresponding responsibilities.

Agents of justice

Onora O'Neill stresses the importance of the perspective of the "agents of justice", i.e., all agents and agencies that can contribute to the construction of justice, play some part in institutionalizing principles of justice or are conformed by them, have been largely neglected in the theoretical debates on global justice, as well as human rights and other global ethics movements (O'Neill 2011, 181). The spotlight on global ethics that was, in part, backed up with the stress on the importance of internationally recognized human rights, was primarily focused on the range and extent of those rights from the beneficiary perspective by claiming their universality, but has left a clear distribution of obligations and responsibilities unclear and underdetermined.

Within such a setting there is a pervasive assumption that the primary agents of justice are states (e.g., since they have the relevant powers to secure basic human rights) and that all other agents are merely secondary or auxiliary agents of justice, in the sense that the latter are "thought to contribute to justice mainly by meeting the demands of primary agents, most evidently by conforming to any legal requirements they establish" (O'Neill 2011, 181). This is highly problematic, especially in the globalized world, where we can see a lot of cases of weak and failed states, which are unable to efficiently play the role of primary agents of justice. The current state is thus that we are faced with a state of affairs where we have a cosmopolitan view of human rights and a statist view of obligations in regard to them.

One way to approach this issue is by focusing on the capabilities and capacities of different agents to contribute to the global system of justice. O'Neill utilizes Amartya Sen's notion of capability in order to move the discussion about obligations and responsibilities for global justice from considerations about the status and motives of different agents to their effective powers, with the hope to achieve a more realistic view of what we can reasonably expect to achieve. Capability is not the same as capacity of power in the abstract and in relation to justice "agents and agencies must dispose, not only of capacities which they could deploy if circumstances were favourable, but of capabilities, that is to say, of *specific, effectively resourced capacities which they can deploy in actual circumstances*" (O'Neill 2011, 189). What is relevant in determining the scope of responsibilities regarding justice are specific capabilities of agents and agencies in concrete situations and not their abstract capacities or their aggregate power

The development of ideal global justice, based on a set of perfectly just institutions "would certainly demand a sovereign global state, and in the absence of such a state, questions of global justice appear to the transcendentalists to be un-addressable" (Sen 2009, 25). However, since such an attitude readily reduces any endeavours towards global justice as an unachievable rhetoric, a more pragmatic approach could prove more useful. Such an approach could be aimed at the abolition of manifest injustices under non-ideal circumstances using a strategy of piecemeal engineering and also focusing on feasible institutional reforms (Mieth 2012, 55). A more comprehensive inclusion of various non-state agents in frameworks for protection of human rights and other aspects of a normative framework of global justice constitutes just this sort of strategic and pragmatic approach.

Hospitality and global justice

The notion of hospitality is becoming more and more present in modern discourse on global ethics. It is employed both in a narrow and a wider sense. In a narrower sense, it is closely connected with moral issues pertaining to the debates and practices regarding immigration and related phenomena (the right of asylum, lawful residence, citizenship, integration, etc.). This area represents an exceptionally important aspect of global ethics, since the scale of these phenomena and related suffering, misery, and frustration are extensive and growing more and more. In 2013, the UN estimated that approximately 232 million people were living abroad as migrants (UN, 2014); in 2000 this number was 175 million and in 1910, it was 33 million (Benhabib 2004, loc. 180). The number of refugees and forcibly displaced people has risen to over 50 million in 2014 (UNHCR 2014). Such a situation opens the grounds for possible conflicts and poses a threat to peace. In this context, the notion of hospitality is key for transgressing the traditional statist framework of exclusive membership based on some supposed national characteristics.

Benhabib stresses the long overlooked importance of political membership in relation to global justice, since a "cosmopolitan theory of justice cannot be restricted to schemes of just distribution on a global scale, but must also incorporate a vision of just membership" (Benhabib 2004, loc. 162–163). After that, she presents a convincing case for a right to hospitality, which will further benefit from the introduction of the mentioned wider normative framework. The right to membership is a human right that can be defended within the principles of morality (Benhabib 2004, loc. 724). She uses the horizon of discourse ethics and Kant's thoughts on cosmopolitan rights (*ius cosmopoliticum*) to establish a positive case for the right of hospitality. The latter puts limits on the sovereignty of states to close off their borders. Defending the right to hospitality and the correlated network of obligations and responsibilities of states and other agents, presents itself as a project of post-national solidarity and "a moral project that transcends existing state boundaries, and nowhere are the tensions between the demands of post-national universalistic solidarity and the practices of exclusive membership more apparent than at the site of territorial borders and boundaries" (Benhabib, 2004, loc. 343–345). What emerges is a more open relationship between temporary residence and (full) membership. A tension or paradox between universal human rights, on the one hand, and sovereignty claims on the other cannot be completely bypassed, but its consequences can be at least, in part, mitigated through the process of democratic iterations of the concept of membership related concepts (Benhabib 2004, loc. 793– 799).

More specifically, starting from Kant's understanding of hospitality, it is not to be understood as a sort of sociable gesture of kindness and generosity, but as a right that belongs to all human beings due to their potential membership in a world republic on the basis of cosmopolitan right (Benhabib 2004, loc. 503–505). Membership is an important aspect since in provides protection. Nowhere has this been more dramatically exposed as in the writing of Hannah Arendt (1962). The role, function or value of a national group and group membership is that it offers an effective protection of an individual's rights. Therefore, Benhabib argues that what we have to leave behind is a strong notion of sovereignty, which includes exclusionary control over the territory, with a model of cosmopolitan rights creating an overlapping network of "obligations and imbrications around sovereignty" (Benhabib, 2004, loc. 1083). One of her main goals was to establish the "assumption that liberal peoples have "fairly open borders"; that they not only permit a fundamental right to emigrate, but that they coexist within a system of mutual obligations and privileges, an essential component of which is the privilege to immigrate, that is, to enter another people's territory and become a member of its society peacefully" (Benhabib 2004, loc. 1418–1421).

Agents of hospitality

An agent of hospitality could be defined as any agent or agency that can contribute to the construction of those aspects of justice (either by playing a part in institutionalizing norms, being conformed by them, contributing so that other agents are conformed by them, or some other type of activity), which are related to the right to hospitality, i.e., all pertinent problems and issues related to membership, emigration and immigration, the right to asylum, the right to residence, etc. One of the key tasks is to formulate a general outline of the duties and responsibilities of these agents regarding the right to hospitality. Among the agents of hospitality, we must first include every agent or agency that has the capability, effective power or decisive influence for protection, promotion and fulfilment of the right to hospitality. Next, these agents can be held responsible and ascribed with both negative and positive duties regarding the right to hospitality. We all accept this for states as agents of hospitality. Organizations other than national states (non-state agents) can be legitimately seen as agents of hospitality, especially in circumstances where they are deeply intertwined with basic institutions and practices of weak or developing states regarding membership and the right to hospitality. Agents other than national states (e.g. transnational organizations, religions and religious communities, NGOs, transnational corporations) can be ascribed with both negative and positive duties regarding the right to hospitality.

What is further needed is a framework to conceptualize different duties and responsibilities of both state and non-state agents. Besides more traditional distinctions like those between positive ones (duties to act in a certain way to achieve x; e.g., protect, promote or fulfil human rights) and negative duties (refraining from acting in a certain way, e.g., refraining from directly violating human rights) or universal ones (applying to all agents of justice at all times) and non-universal duties (not owned by all agents of justice); we must find further ways to lay foundations for a more complex structure of human rights protection, and especially the right to hospitality, in the light of global justice (cf. Kolstad, 2007). This structure must be such to be able to accommodate questions regarding different agents of justice and their priority position in this system of protection, the extent of their possible human rights duties, differences between particular human rights and the time perspective of their respect, protection and fulfilment.

Religions and hospitality

Religious communities and religions in general are also an important agents of hospitality. Kearney (2010) contrast "hostility" as the violent potential of religion with "hospitality" or healing potential of religion as the antidote for it and relates both to imagination as the resource and mechanism, which shapes our attitudes and actions. One frequent common aspect of religions is the moment of the encounter with a "Stranger" usually related to the Holy One, in which an individual or a community in light of religious reflection, hermeneutic (and with this non-fundamentalist) discernment and imagination overcome the initial response of fear and respond with a gesture of hospitality and welcome. In order to be able to do that some level of radical initial trust must be established (Kearney 2010, 16–17). In encountering the Stranger one faces her or him as defenceless, vulnerable, as calling for justice and asking us to receive it in our midst (Kearney 2010, 18–19). "The Stranger, in short, is the uninvited one who has nowhere to lay his head unless we act as hosts and provide a dwelling place. There is a sense of radical surprise and irruption about the coming of this estranged and estranging outsider – a sense of unknowability calling for risk and adventure on our part. Hospitality to the radical other does not come naturally. It requires imagination and faith" (Kearney 2010, 19).

Religions thus have a vital role in establishing hospitality and in the process of overcoming new religious intolerance by creating a context of sympathetic imagination and respect. This also represents our willingness to step out of our ego and enter into the world of the other. This allows us to avoid the phenomenon of "invisible other" or "invisible others" (Nussbaum 2012, 139–140). A special challenge for such a sympathetic imagination is that the other is often different or distant, which means we must first make the other real for us. Inclusive imagination and sympathy represent only one aspect of compassion and care, but they are crucial, because they are moving us in the opposite direction as fear, that is in the direction of the other. Narcissism misleads us, when it persuades us that we can go through our life with other people, not to make any efforts in the domain of imagination, sympathy and care, and this is one of the main forms of moral error (Nussbaum 2012, 169). It degenerates into the form that recognizes the laws protecting rights as applicable only to ourselves, thus denying the reality of the other and his/her equality. Compassionate empathy and imagination are able to overcome such tunnel vision or blind spots, and do that in a way that mere arguments cannot, because the former include experiential participation (solidarity) on/with the other, but it also goes beyond it, since it evaluates, criticizes and explores the values that are embedded in the situation, and to dismantles hierarchies, stigmatization and undeserved suffering. Such compassion must be based on truth because only the truth helps us to overcome our narcissistic fantasies and represents the basis for civil friendship and insight into the full humanity of the other (Nussbaum 2012, 186–187). On such a basis we can develop an empathic society of hospitality and dialogue (Juhant and Strahovnik 2011; Strahovnik 2015b).

As for the religious communities their duties and responsibilities are more concrete. As active members of the civil societies they can contribute a public debate, public opinion and attitudes, and consequently legislation of justice regarding the hospitality. Many religious communities have done this in relation to the recent refugee and immigration situation in Europe. Next, in relation to the capabilities of enacting of justice regarding the hospitality they have responsibilities to respond to concrete needs of affected individuals. Lynch thus rightly argues that an array of various agents related to peacebuilding today "includes religious communities, which themselves include churches, mosques, temples, other sacred communities and sites, religiously supported nongovernmental organizations, mission organizations, intra- and interfaith organizations (local, national, and transnational) …" (Lynch 2015, 599), since hospitality and peacebuilding efforts are often interconnected and overlapping in relation to global justice.

Conclusion

The questions of membership, immigration, and hospitality are one of the most pertinent questions within the scheme of cosmopolitan justice. In relation to the European Union (and other parts of the world also), the waves of refugees and other immigrants trying to reach and cross its borders, and the associated death toll, suffering and frustration on the one side and reactions of the EU population on the other that we are witnessing daily are a painful example of this. Given the pertinent global need to address the issues related to membership, immigration and, especially, refugee status and asylum, this project is one of the central projects for cosmopolitan ethics and the ethics of hospitality. That is why it is so important to focus our attention on the notion of hospitality and conceptualize a wider network of agents of hospitality together with corresponding duties and obligations. Only a joint effort of these agents could pave the way for progress towards cosmopolitan justice, embodying the genuine, peaceful ethics of hospitality. In this joint effort religions and religious communities have a vital role to play. The proposal in this paper aims exactly towards this aim.

REFERENCES

Appiah, K. A. 2007. *Cosmopolitanism: Ethics in a World of Strangers*. London: Penguin Books.

Audi, R. 2007. *Moral Value and Human Diversity*. New York: Oxford University Press.

Benhabib, S. 2004. *The Rights of Others*. Cambridge: Cambridge University Press. Kindle Edition.

Benhabib, S. 2011. *Dignity in Adversity. Human Rights for Troubled Times*. Cambridge: Polity Press.

Juhant, J. & Strahovnik, V. 2011. Ali je možna empatična družba dialoga? [Is an empathic society of dialogue possible?]. *Bogoslovni vestnik* 71, 495–509.

Kearney, R. 2010. Imagining the Sacred Stranger. Hostility or Hospitality. In: Dyck, J., Rowe, P. & Zimmermann, J. (eds) *Politics and the Religious Imagination*. New York: Routledge, pp. 15–30.

Kolstad. I. 2007. Human Rights and Assigned Duties: Implications for Corporations. CMI Working Papers 7, 1–11. Http://www.cmi.no/publications/file/2814-human-rights-and-assigned-duties.pdf (15. 9. 2014)

Lynch. C. 2015. Religious Communities and Possibilities for Justpeace. In: Omer, A. Appleby,R.S. & Little, D. (eds) *The Oxford Handbook of Religion, Conflict, and Peacebuilding*. New York: Oxford University Press, 597-612.

Mieth, C. 2012. Global Injustice, Individual Duties and Non-ideal Institutional Circumstances. *Civitas*, 12(1), 47–69.

Nagel, T. 2005. The Problem of Global Justice. *Philosophy & Public Affairs* 33(2): 113–147.

Nussbaum, M. 2006a. *Creating Capabilites. The Human Development Approach*. Cambridge, MA: The Belknap Press of Harvard University Press.

Nussbaum, M. 2006b. *Frontiers of Justice: Disability, Nationality, Species Membership*. Cambridge, MA: Belknap Press of Harvard University Press.

Nussbaum, M. 2012. *The New Religious Intolerance: Overcoming the Politics of Fear in an Anxious Age*. Cambridge, MA: The Belknap Press.

O'Neill, O. 2000. *Bounds of Justice*. Cambridge: Cambridge University Press.

O'Neill, O. 2005. The Dark Side of Human Rights. *International Affairs*, 81(2), 427–439.

O'Neill, O. 2011. Agents of Justice. *Metaphilosophy*, 32(1/2), 180–195.

Pogge, T. W. 2002. *World Poverty and Human Rights*. Cambridge: Polity Press.

Sen, A. 2009. *The Idea of Justice*. Cambridge, MA: Belknap Press.

Singer, P. 2004. *One World: The Ethics of Globalization*. New Haven: Yale University Press.

Strahovnik, V. 2015. Corporations as Agents of Global Justice. In: Letnar Černič, J. & T. van Ho (eds): *Human rights and business: direct corporate accountability for human rights.* Oisterwijk: Wolf Legal Publishers, 161–178.

Strahovnik, V. 2015b. Global justice and agents of hospitality. *Annales,* 25(2), 253–262,

UN 2014. 232 million international migrants living abroad worldwide: New UN global migration statistics reveal. Http://esa.un.org/unmigration/wallchart2013.htm (15. 9. 2014).

UNHCR 2014. Facts and Figures about Refugees. Http://www.unhcr.org.uk/about-us/key-facts-and-figures.html (15. 9. 2014).

van Hooft, S. 2009. *Cosmopolitanism. A Philosophy for Global Ethics*. Stocksfield: Acumen.

ABSTRACTS

Janez Juhant

From ideological pressure to the sound policy of cooperation

Abstract: The article deals with a "renaissance" of religions, which concerns the impact of religion in society, interest in religion among scientists (especially among sociologists and political theorists), and the growing role of religions in international relations. This opens a question whether religions are a source of violence. The liberal tensions in the society of modernity caused polarization, and religions were often victims of these processes, although also taking part in it. Following this development, sociologists more and more acknowledge the importance of religions in the socio-political sphere. The article points at the influence of dominant and totalitarian thinking on the (negative) role of religions in society. We have witnessed a global political development in the direction of concentration of the whole political power by particular political entities and persons. This culminated in the totalitarian systems. They extinguish differentiated (ambiguity; Bauer 2014) classic human, cultural and ethical order. In extreme-revolutionary circumstances, the traditional values were suspended and – in the communist countries – "non-values" (laying, stealing, murdering) prevailed. These tendencies have overcame Islam too. 'Violence' is a general anthropological problem and only a dialogical society can solve it, including violence related to the religious area.

Keywords: religion, politics, liberalism, totalitarianism, Christianity, Islam, religious freedom, Eucharistic community.

Bojan Žalec

Radical Islamism and Totalitarianism

Abstract: The author argues that radical Islamism is a totalitarian attitude and movement. The chief aim of this essay is to explain in which sense ideologies and groups of radical Islamism can be called totalitarian, and what form of totalitarianism they exemplify. In the analysis of the totalitarian aspects of radical Islamism, the theory of Hannah Arendt is applied. It turns out, on one hand, that the central elements of the secular totalitarianisms stressed by Arendt are present in radical Islamism but also, on the other hand, that some specific characteristics of it can be noticed.

Keywords: Radical Islamism, totalitarianism, violence, terror, ideology.

Lenart Škof

Faith and Humility: On the Future of Theology of Religions

Abstract: This essay is an attempt to think a new theory of religion based on two Western thinkers – Wilfred Cantwell Smith, a Canadian theologian and religious scholar, and Roberto Mangabeira Unger, Brazilian-American pragmatist scholar (a professor of law at Harvard and a philosopher of religion). The aim of this essay first is to define the principle task of our time, and for that purpose we begin with Peter Sloterdijk's recent book *You must change your life* (*Du Mußt dein Leben ändern*). We argue for a more critical approach towards recent philosophical theories of religion and argue for a new constellation, being able to inaugurate both – new theology of religion of Smith's type as well as new pragmatist philosophy of religion of Unger, later being also infused with an air of political and social ethics. With this essay, we finally wish to affirm a need for religion in our time, based on two main 'virtues' – on faith and humility.

Keywords: faith, humility, W.C. Smith, theology of religions, religious exclusivism, interreligious dialogue, R.M. Unger, American pragmatism, religion of the future, P. Sloterdijk, G.E. Lessing.

Branko Klun

Metaphysics, Violence, and Vattimo's Postmodern Democracy

Abstract: The article, which mainly deals with Gianni Vattimo's hermeneutical and political thought, first provides a reconstruction of his critique of metaphysics that was largely inspired by Heidegger. Here, metaphysics is interpreted as a way of thinking which is intrinsically linked to violence, and Vattimo also recognises the remnants of metaphysical violence in the prevailing political system of liberal democracy. His critique of liberal democracy and his ideal of a hermeneutic democracy are presented in the second part of the article. The conclusion consists of some critical reflections on Vattimo's position, and urges for a rehabilitation of the notion of truth, as well as for a more positive interpretation of metaphysics.

Keywords: Vattimo, hermeneutic democracy, metaphysics, violence, postmodernism.

Sandra Lehmann

Overcoming the Will-to-Power. John Milbank's Discussion of Ontological Violence

Abstract: In my view, it is true, as Milbank writes in the preface to the second edition of "Theology and Social Theory", that "a theological vision alone [can] challenge the emerging hegemony of neo-liberalism." Yet, I

disagree with the basic structure of Milbank's project. As I will show, there is a certain Nietzscheanism to it even if or, actually, especially because it presents itself as some sort of Counter-Nietzscheanism. In contrast, I will propose a different ontological approach. Methodologically, unlike Milbank, I will not focus on the link between narrativity and practical implementation. Rather, far more material and realist, my starting point will be the experience of suffering. As it refers both to integrity as well as to the reliance on others, radical orthodox key concepts such as mutuality and peace have to be based on it.
Keywords: Radical Orthodoxy, John Milbank, violence, ontology, metaphysics, political theology.

Mario Wintersteiger
The Beneficial Poison of Mythology. Reflections on Georges Bataille's Anthropology of Myth and Violence
Abstract: When being confronted with myth and violence, the 'politically correct' taboos of the mainstream of political philosophy and its lack of anthropological knowledge become obvious. Trying to avoid these shortcomings, our reflections focus on Georges Bataille and his writings on the sublime and the sacral. Following some of his insights into the psychology of the Fascist appeal to the masses and his meditations on a certain fascination with violence, we point out that it can be politically dangerous to misjudge the power of myth. Since it cannot be wholly banned, there seems to be a need for other ways of protecting us from its most toxic and violent forms. Following Bataille and Michel Maffesoli's sociology, we conclude that small, controlled doses of mythology can have the effect of a beneficial poison that immunises people against the more dangerous myths.
Keywords: anthropology, political philosophy, Georges Bataille, mythology, violence.

Nadja Furlan Štante
"Power Over" Hierarchical Domination: A Stem Cell of Violence
Abstract: Paper understands the hierarchical supremacy and the battle for the (pre) power in the terms of "power over" and domination between the genders as a key or stem cell of gender-based violence. Negative gender stereotypes and prejudices are understood as promoters and preservers of hierarchical supremacy and of the battle for the (pre) power between the genders. Using the methodology of hermeneutic key of feminist theology attempts to warn of the danger and harmfulness of negative gender stereotypes and prejudices and the link between them and gender-based violence, including

physical (sexual) violence. With the help of quick and short insight into the headlines that are understood as flashy taboos of contemporary Slovenian society, paper briefly analyzes the situation in Slovenian socio-religious sphere. At the end, the ideal of the logic of love against the logic of domination is presented.
Keywords: religion, gender, hierarchical supremacy, sexual violence.

Rok Svetlič

The Communist Hypothesis and the Second Vatican Council

Abstract: In this paper, the radical political philosophy will be discussed (A. Badiou, S. Žižek). The philosophy of religion – since it enables the sight on the totality of the Being – will be used as the meta-position that enables the recognition of the structure of ideology and its affinity to violence. It will be demonstrated that certain ideological concepts are very similar to the understanding of the Being that was characteristic for the medieval Christianity. Its key-problem is the boundary between the holiness of specific places, persons, objects on one hand, and the rest of the world on the other. Similarly, A. Badiou insists on the absolute exclusion of the truth out of the democracy. If the democratic culture insists on the ideal of the reconcilability of antagonisms, this attitude for the communist hypothesis is the treachery of the truth. It will be demonstrated that the radical political philosophy lacks the fundamental and honest reconsolidation with the world.
Keywords: A. Badiou, S. Žižek, violence, medieval Christianity.

Vojko Strahovnik

Religion, Global Justice and Hospitality

Abstract: The paper addresses selected dimensions of global justice debate, especially those that are connected with the concept of hospitality. It introduces and elaborates the concept of agents of justice. This then enables one to approach the notion of hospitality, and within a global justice context, to address some open questions. The importance of those questions is demonstrated with the work of Seyla Benhabib and her defence of the right to hospitality. All this then paves the way to develop a notion of agents of hospitality, which include religions and religious communities. Religions are important source for a proper understanding of dimensions of hospitality, while religious communities harbour capacities to enact it.
Key words: global ethics, global justice, cosmopolitan justice, agents of justice, religions, religious communities, hospitality.

REVIEWS

The book Religion, Violence, and Ideology: Reflections on the Challenges of Postmodern World is an engaging collection of essays dealing with the topic of violence and how to overcome it. It features nine contributions by some leading authors in the field resulting in a comprehensive and well structured investigation of the subject. The essays are accompanied by an editors' introduction that briefly announces the contributions and structures them in a wider framework of the debate. The book tackles the topics of religion as a possible source of violence, anthropological foundations of violence, postmodern context of violence (totalitarianism, fundamentalism, propaganda, secularism, global challenges, ideological terror, weak notion of the truth, etc.), but moreover proposes solutions and a way forward, both on the level of an individual as well as society as a whole (ethics of hospitality, recognition of vulnerability, overcoming gender prejudices, culture of peace). In conclusion, I can affirm that the book Religion, Violence, and Ideology is an original scientific contribution presenting an appealing collection of essays tackling interesting aspects of postmodern condition form the perspective of theology and philosophy. The included essays are informative, engaging, and motivating. The collection as a whole is of interest and may be recommended to academic scholars as well as advanced students in the field.

dr. Rafal Smoczynski, Institute of Philosophy and Sociology of the Polish Acedemy of Sciences, Warsaw, Poland

Avtorji v monografiji odpirajo vrsto izvirnih znanstveno formuliranih vprašanj, obenem pa ponujajo tudi številna nova spoznanja, ki izvirajo iz njihovih lastnih raziskav. Konceptualizacija in razumevanje religije, ideologije in nasilja zlasti v zadnjem času zbujajo ne le pozornost najširše javnosti, temveč kličejo tudi k poglobljeni znastveni obravnavi. Ker so fenomeni religije, nasilja in ideologije izrazito kompleksni in večplastni, to zahteva interdisciplinarni pristop. Tej zahtevi monografija ne le zadosti, temveč jo tudi preseže, saj ponuja poglobljeno filozofsko, teološko in religiološko perspektivo razmisleka. V celoti gledano je monografija znanstveno pomembna predvsem za področje humanistike pa tudi za napredek v interdisciplinarnem raziskovanju njene problematike.

Pred svetom, Evropo ter našo državo in družbo so veliki problemi in naloge, ki so v znatni meri takšne narave, da so raziskave in zamisli, s katerimi se ukvarja zadevna monografija, bistvenega pomena, saj so pravilno razumevanje, opredeljevanje in ovrednotenje religije z vidika ideologije in nasilja, pogojev, dejavnikov, vzrokov in učinkov teh pojavov ter njihove kulturno-primerjalne raziskave odločilnega pomena za spoprijemanje z najbolj perečimi problemi sodobnega sveta. Povedano je razvidno že samo, če se spomnimo na z verskimi vojnami prepleteno evropsko zgodovino in izredno zaskrbljujočo težo problematike religiozno zaznamovanega fundamentalizma, terorizma in nasilja na splošno v sedanjosti. Z vidika splošno kulturnih, ideoloških, religioznih, političnih in drugih razlik sodbne globalne družbe sodi tematika monografije v tem trenutku med najaktualnejše naloge humanistike.

Izrazoslovje v monografiji je zelo bogato, v njej pa so na izviren in znanstveno prepričljiv način analizirani in aplicirani številni pojmi, uporabljajoč različne pristope – od fenomenološkega, hermenevtičnega do religiološkega. Delo odlikuje visoka raven kakovostne zgoščene obravnave in sintetiziranja različnih pogledov in pristopov ter hkrati tudi zmožnost njihovega kritičnega pretresa. Poudariti kaže tudi pomemben prispevek monografije h kritičnemu razmisleku in možnemu oblikovanju postsekularne culture, primerne za sodobni svet. Zato lahko utemeljeno trdim, da ocenjevana monografija predstavlja zelo pomemben prispevek k sodobni humanistiki, družboslovju in interdisciplinarnosti; vsekakor tudi v svetovnem merilu.

Monografija je napisana na vrhunski znanstveni ravni. Kot taka seveda ne more biti v celoti in v podrobnostih dostopna širšemu krogu bralcev. Vendar pa so lahko njene osrednje zamisli, ugotovitve in sporočila razumljiva in koristna tudi za te bralce, med katere vsekakor ne spadajo samo duhovniki in učitelji ter študentje veroslovnih in religioloških predmetov, ampak tudi učitelji filozofije, sociologije, etike in sorodnih šolskih predmetov, socialni delavci, vojaki, policisti in ne nazadnje politiki. Ne gre pa pozabiti niti dejstva, da se z izdajo pri pomembni tuji založbi določen del vplivnih slovenskih humanistov in družboslovcev na ta način predstavlja svetovni javnosti. Menim, da si zadevna monografija vsekakor zasluži finančno podporo ARRS.

Full Prof. Ciril Sorč, Faculty of Theology, University of Ljubljana, Slovenia

AUTHORS

Nadja Furlan Štante, PhD, is Senior Research Fellow at the Science and Research Centre, University of Primorska, and Associate Professor of Religious Studies at the Faculty of Humanities, University of Primorska, Slovenia.

Janez Juhant, Prof. Emeritus at the Faculty of Theology, University of Ljubljana, Slovenia, and a member of the European Academy of Sciences and Arts in Salzburg.

Branko Klun is an Associate Professor of Philosophy at the Faculty of Theology, University of Ljubljana, Slovenia.

Sandra Lehmann is an Assistant Professor at the Catholic Private University Linz, Austria.

Vojko Strahovnik is an Assistant Professor and Research Associate at the Faculty of Theology, University of Ljubljana, Slovenia.

Rok Svetlič, PhD, is an Associate Professor and researcher at the Scientific and Research Centre, University of Primorska, Slovenia.

Lenart Škof is a researcher and the head of the Institute for Philosophical Studies, University of Primorska, and a professor at the Faculty of Theology, University of Ljubljana, Slovenia.

Mario Wintersteiger is a Lecturer at the University of Salzburg, Austria.

Bojan Žalec is an Associate Professor of Philosophy and Senior Research Fellow, Faculty of Theology, University of Ljubljana, Slovenia. He is the Head of the Institute of Philosophy and Social Ethics at the same faculty.